Landscapes of the
SCOTTISH HIGHLANDS
and the Isle of Skye

a countryside guide

Stephen Whitehorne

SUNFLOWER BOOKS

Dedicated to Gran

First published 1999
by Sunflower Books™
12 Kendrick Mews
London SW7 3HG, UK

ISBN 1-85691-130-6

Piper at Glen Coe (Car tour 4)

Important note to the reader

We have tried to ensure that the descriptions and maps in this book are error-free at press date. The book will be updated, where necessary, whenever future printings permit. It will be very helpful for us to receive your comments (sent in care of the publishers, please) for the updating of future printings.

We also rely on those who use this book — especially walkers — to take along a good supply of common sense when they explore. Conditions change fairly rapidly in Scotland, and **storm damage, tree-felling, avalanche risk or ice may make a route unsafe at any time**. If the route is not as we outline it here, and your way ahead is not secure, return to the point of departure. **Never attempt to complete a tour or walk under hazardous conditions!** Please read carefully the notes on pages 45-50, as well as the introductory comments at the beginning of each tour and walk (regarding road conditions, equipment, grade, distances and time, etc). Explore **safely**, while at the same time respecting the beauty of the countryside.

Cover photograph: Arrochar Alps from Loch Arklet at Inversnaid (Car tour 1, Walk 4)
Title page: Scots pines in Glen Falloch (Car tour 2)
Photographs by the author
Maps reproduced from 1998 Landranger 1:50,000 Ordnance Survey maps by permission of Ordnance Survey on behalf of Her Majesty's Stationery Office, © Crown Copyright MC 027017.
A CIP catalogue record for this book is available from the British Library.
Printed and bound in the UK by Brightsea Press, Exeter

10 9 8 7 6 5 4 3 2

Contents

Walking 45

Index 134

Useful addresses/STOP PRESS 136

Fold-out touring map *inside back cover*

 Preface

Early in 1991, I turned my back on life in London and took up a post as a photography tutor at the other end of Britain. On the global scale of things, relocating 650km/400mi further north might not seem too big a step to take, but that shock — from crowded capital to highland seclusion — could not have been more abrupt. And anyone who believes England and Scotland (just because they are both in Britain) are really the one and same place should think again!

The vastness of the countryside that I was immersed in at Inversnaid, on the 'Bonnie Banks' of Loch Lomond, was at first difficult to take in, but I quickly came to love this new landscape. Since then, by continually exploring the nooks and crannies as well as the mountaintops, my passion for the Scottish Highlands has intensified. This wilderness gives me not only the fresh air and physical rejuvenation that I crave, but it affects me on a far more profound level as well, providing endless poetic and aesthetic inspiration for my work as a photographer. The region's social and natural history is fascinating, but this landscape can be an essential spiritual refuge too.

Compared to many other titles in the series, *Landscapes of the Scottish Highlands* covers a vast geographical area, over half of Scotland in fact. Geologically speaking, the Scottish Highlands can be defined as the mountainous area which lies north of the Highland Boundary Fault. This fault line dissects the southern half of Loch Lomond and forms The Trossachs. Somewhat confusingly, the administrative region called Highland Region lies north of this line, having its southern boundary roughly along a line between Glen Etive and the Cairngorm Mountains. For the purpose of this book, the geological definition is more appropriate.

Visitors to Scotland are often surprised to discover that there are no national parks here. Until recently the land has not suffered from the pressures of population, or the problems of access that are common in many other parts of Europe. However, due to its increasing importance as a recreational resource, plans are currently underway to establish Loch Lomond and The Trossachs as the country's first national park, with possibly the Cairngorms area to follow. Another surprise, when venturing into the Highlands for the first time, is the experience of a landscape mostly devoid of trees (forestry plantations aside). This is not a new situation, the native pine forests of Caledon having been plundered for centuries to satisfy man's insatiable demand for agricultural land and for timber for fuel, shipbuilding and various war efforts. When Dr Johnston made his famous tour of Scotland in 1713, he remarked that 'a tree in Scotland was as rare as a horse in Venice'.

In many ways, the Highland landscape is now an ecological wasteland, an empty wilderness, where the wolf, elk and brown bear once roamed. Often described as a vast wet desert, it is a desert today interspersed with false green oases — the coniferous regiments of forestry plantations mostly made up of non-native tree species. But this is only part of the very long story about an amazingly diverse and ancient landscape, one shaped both by natural and human forces.

The most recent geological shaping of the land occurred as a result of glacial action during the last ice age, 10,000 years ago. Huge sheets of ice gouged out the corries, cut back the narrow crests of mountains and broadened the valleys between them. But the geological story stretches back much further still; the mountains of Scotland are made up of some of the oldest rocks in the world.

Now one of the most sparsely-settled areas of Europe, the Highlands were once far more populated. The history of human communities in Scotland stretches back some 8500 years, although the most likely evidence of habitations that you will encounter on your walks are the ruined remains of deserted cottages and villages from the 18th and 19th centuries. Scattered throughout the glens, they are the sad testimony to the tragedy of the Highland clearances. After the breakdown of the clan system, the people were forcibly evicted by the new landlords in order to establish more profitable sheep and deer estates.

Today a stark and dramatic beauty characterises one of Europe's last great wilderness areas, one of the few remaining landscapes where genuine solitude can be sought and where the luxuries of silence and space abound.

Finally, before going any further, it is perhaps worth dispelling a few myths about Scotland. Most men here do not wear kilts, and you are only ever likely to see the wearing of traditional Highland garb, or the playing of the bagpipes, at the tourist hot-spots or at special ceremonies such as weddings. Remember too that the heather of the open moors is only purple in August, when it flowers. Romantic, medieval castles are numerous throughout the Highlands, but most are in a ruinous state. And before you pack your binoculars and long camera lenses, it is as well to know that Nessie-watching is considered a certifiable-condition! Yet despite all the tourist board hype perpetuating these myths, survey after survey reveals that most people visit Scotland for the reality, for the beauty and great diversity of its scenery, to discover remote lochs, atmospheric glens and dramatic mountains. The car tours, picnics and walks in this book will allow you to discover the very best the Highlands have to offer, whether from your driving seat, out on a short stroll or committed to an energetic mountain climb.

Acknowledgements

For taking care of things while I was just too preoccupied with putting this book together to notice the domestic chaos descending upon me, I once again have to thank Virginie for all her support. Also, had I relied on my own keyboard skills rather than hers to produce the manuscript, I doubt this book would have seen the shop shelves before the next millennium!

Each one of my walking companions has shown amazing patience whenever I plunged yet again into my rucksack for the Dictaphone, for film or for the right lens. I thank Donny McCleod, Simon Mootz, Clare Henderson, Dave Ruff and Séverine Bernalin for their continued friendship.

The advice and tips which come from talking to local people is the best kind and can never be sourced in books. Conversations with André Gaulancourt, Linda Middleton and John Barrington have proved invaluable in furthering my knowledge and fostering my passion for the environment around Inversnaid and the Southern Highlands. Tam Bolton of the Luib Hotel had some useful suggestions in Glen Dochart, as did the proprietor of Drumnadrochit Guest House regarding walks in the vicinity of Braemar. My first visit to the wilds of Sutherland was both a beautiful and a daunting experience; it was difficult to know just where to start walking until a chat with the friendly SNH staff at the Knockan Cliff Visitor Centre helped me to devise two of the best possible routes in Assynt.

For accommodating me on the Isle of Skye I cannot thank enough Anne and Roy Robinson, whose generosity I shall never forget. The driver of the Postbus to Elgol was also great company, that morning before I began the long walk back to Sligachan, divulging, as he delivered the mail, amusing tales on subjects ranging from Bonnie Prince Charlie's adventures on Skye to his own TV fame with the BBC. Also, for the use of the loveliest of little cottages by the sea, I am grateful to Mrs Mackenzie of Port Henderson. For tea and chat at the end of a rainy day in Glen Lyon, I thank Kate Conway at the Bridge of Balgie post office. Finally, I thank my publisher, Pat Underwood of Sunflower Books, for all her advice and support.

Glossary

In keeping with general language use in Scotland, I have used the Gaelic words* ben (mountain), glen (valley) and loch (lake) throughout this book. I have also used a few other words specific to describing features in Scotland: bothy — cottage or hut; burn — stream or brook; croft — small farmstead. It is also worth remembering that in Scotland, mountains are generally referred to as hills. *A hillwalker therefore is someone who climbs mountains.* To avoid constant repetition, a limited number of abbreviations have been used in the walk descriptions.

Abbreviations

FC — Forestry Commission
OS — Ordnance Survey
NNR — National Nature Reserve
NTS — National Trust for Scotland
RSPB — Royal Society for the Protection of Birds
WHW — West Highland Way
YH — Youth Hostel

Gaelic names

aber — mouth of loch, river
abhainn — river
allt — stream
aonach — ridge
auch, ach — field
bal, bail — town, homestead
ban — white, fair, pale
bealach — hill pass
beg, beag — small
ben, beinn — hill
bhuidhe — yellow
bidean — pinnacle
blar — plain
brae, braigh — upper slope, steepening
breac — speckled
cam — cam
cairn — pile of stones, often marking a summit
carn — cairn, cairn-shaped hill

caol, kyle — strait
ceann, kin, ken — head
ciche, cioch — breast, breast-shaped hill
cil, kil — church, cell
clach — stone
cnoc — hill, knoll
coillie, killie — wood
corrie, coire, choire — mountain hollow
creag, craig — cliff, crag
dal, dail — field, flat
damh– stag
dearg — red
druim, drum — long ridge
dubh, dhu — black, dark
dun — hill fort
eas — waterfall
eilean — island
eilidh — hind
eun — bird
fada — long
fionn — white
fraoch — heather
gabhar, ghabhar, gobhar — goat
garbh — rough
geal — white
gearr — short
glen, gleann — narrow valley
glias, glas — grey
gorm — blue, green
inch, inis — island, meadow by river
inver, inbhir — confluence

ken, kin — head
kyle — strait
lag, laggan — hollow
larach — old site
lairig — broad pass
leac — slab
liath — grey
loch — lake (diminutive: *lochan*)
mam — pass, rise
maol — bare or bald (normally refers to mountaintop without vegetation)
meall — mound
monadh — upland
mór(e) — big
odhar, odhair — dun-coloured
rhu, rubha — point
riabhach — brindled or striped
ruadh — red, brown
sgor, sgurr — pointed
sneachd — snow
sron — nose
stob — pointed
strath — valley (wider than glen)
tarmachan — ptarmigan
tarsuinn — transverse, across
tom — hillock (rounded)
torr — hillock (more rugged)
tulloch, tulach — knoll
uaine — green, pallid
uisge — water, river

*Gaelic words not commonly found in British dictionaries are italicised.

Getting about

Using public transport in the Scottish Highlands can be an extremely frustrating and very time-consuming way of getting about. It is also an expensive way to travel compared to many other parts of Europe. That said, it can have its own joys, especially if you intend using the Postbus services. But if you would rather spend the bulk of your limited time exploring the Highlands on foot, and at your own pace, then the use of a **car** is essential.

Visitors from other parts of Britain and from continental Europe will, more often than not, travel to Scotland overland in their own vehicles. Those arriving in the country at the railway stations and airports will not have to look far to find the offices of all the major car hire companies. You can hire a **taxi** for one-off journeys in the Highlands, although these can be expensive if you are travelling alone, and the fare is rarely negotiable.

Coach tours are an option for visiting the more popular sights over one or two days. They provide a painless introduction to the Highland scenery and a taste of what to expect on the roads.

Railways are now all but non-existent in the Scottish Highlands and so, with the exception of services to a few large towns such as Oban, Fort William and Inverness, train travel is not a viable option. Therefore, for the most part, you will have to rely on **bus** and **coach services**. Most of the main towns and villages of the Highlands are served by the big operators from Scotland's cities. Coaches, normally one or two daily and running on time, leave Edinburgh, Glasgow, Perth, Stirling and Dundee for the north. The Cairngorms and Deeside can be reached by services to and from Aberdeen, while the Northern Highlands are served mainly by coaches from Inverness. These trunk routes are operated by Scottish Citylink, Stage Coach and one or two other companies.

A number of smaller bus companies, such as Midland Bluebird (Southern Highlands), Gaelic Bus (Lochaber), Wester Bus (Wester Ross) and Skyeways (Skye) operate the **country bus** services in particular localities. These run at varying levels of frequency and reliability. However, it is the **Postbuses** that serve the remoter areas of the Highlands, providing a lifeline for many rural communities. There are more than 140 Postbus routes in Scotland, but you will need to study their timetables carefully to plan walks around them. Also, because they normally stop at every house en route to deliver mail, journeys can be lengthy — but they will deposit you *exactly* where you want to be dropped off. Postbuses carry both passengers and mail, may be up to 15-seater vehicles and are bright red. There are *no* Postbuses operating on Sundays, and very few other local buses.

Up-to-date timetables for local and Postbus services can be obtained from tourist information offices. Telephone numbers for the major bus and train operators are listed on page 136.

Lake and Port of Menteith (Car tour 1, Picnic 1)

❀ Picnicking

There are very few official picnic sites in the Scottish Highlands. Those that do exist are invariably beside main roads and in summer can be crowded and noisy places. Most of my twelve suggestions that are listed below involve a bit more effort to find seclusion, although none will involve more than a 35-minute walk from your car. These are simply idyllic spots that I have discovered for myself. Almost anywhere you decide to picnic in the Scottish Highlands is going to be a good place to eat out!

For each car tour I have highlighted at least one picnic suggestion; some of the settings are located along the routes of the walks. All of the picnics which involve some walking make excellent short walks in themselves.

Food somehow always tastes better outdoors, which is fortunate — since Scottish cuisine is often far from imaginative. Stodgy foods are pretty much the order of the day in the Highlands. It is a good idea to stock up with your favourite nibbles before you leave the city, as choice in rural grocery stores can be extremely limited. Obviously, in relation to perishable foods, you will, before long, have to seek out what you can locally. Take advantage of buying fresh fruit and vegetables wherever you find them and remember: nearly all grocery stores in the Highlands will be closed on Sundays.

When eating out, bar meals in pubs and hotels are the least expensive option, however, you might soon find yourselves overdosing on breaded haddock, chips and peas. Scottish salmon and seafood, revered the world over, is strangely lacking in all but the most salubrious establishments.

All picnickers should read the Country code on page 46 and go quietly in the countryside.

1 ISLAND PARADISE

Car tour 1: Park off the B8034 at **Port of Menteith** (photograph opposite) and take the passenger ferry (April-September) out to **Inchmahome Priory**. After just a few minutes, you disembark by the lawn at the remains of this priory, the best spot on the island to picnic. From this tranquil wooded refuge in the middle of the Lake of Menteith, you may be lucky enough to see ospreys. Outside the summer season, there are numerous picnicking alternatives — use the car parks in the **Duke's Pass** or on the road out to **Inversnaid** (photographs pages 18 and 61).

11

2 ON THE SEAT OF CAMPBELL CHIEFS

Car tour 2: **Kilchurn Castle**, overlooking the extensive waters and little islets of Loch Awe, was once the headquarters of the powerful Campbells of Argyll. These quietly-evocative remains are now under the stewardship of Historic Scotland and can be reached in 15 minutes from the main road (A85; photograph page 21). Other very fine picnic places include the '**Rest and be Thankful**', on Dun na Cuaiche, beside the River Orchy, at **Inverarnan** and at **Inveruglas**.

3 WHERE ALPINE FLOWERS GROW

Car tour 3: The alpine nature reserve at **Ben Lawers**, on the banks of the Burn of Edramucky, is at the beginning of Walk 10. You can park at the National Trust Visitor Centre on Ben Lawers. Follow the path over the boardwalk, cross the stile, and venture into the reserve as far as you like, taking care of course not to crush the rare and beautiful alpine flowers which flourish here. Allow up to 20 minutes to find your ideal spot on the grass. Numerous possibilities for picnicking can also be found in **Glen Lyon** (photograph page 24) or **Glen Lochay**, at gaps in the trees beside their lovely rivers.

4 IN THE SHADOW OF THE BIG BEN

Car tour 4: In summer at least, car parks and official picnic sites in the Lochaber area can become incredibly crowded. For seclusion, it is better to be prepared to walk short distances. It is difficult to imagine a more idyllic spot than on the meadow above the Nevis Gorge, by the **Steall Waterfall** (photograph page 83). Follow Walk 12 (page 82) for 30 minutes, from the end of the Glen Nevis road.

5 ON THE DEVIL'S STAIRCASE

Car tour 4: Park at Altnafeadh, at the top of Glen Coe. A good footpath (the WHW) goes north and zigzags up the '**Devil's Staircase**'. (The path got this name during the 1800s, when navies working on the dam at Blackwater Reservoir would stagger back in a drunken stupor from the King's House Hotel and, on more than one occasion, fell and died of exposure here.) At the top of the staircase, a 35-minute climb from the road, there is a view of Ben Nevis and the Mamores which, for such a short walk, is impossible to match anywhere else. The least- frequented roadside option for a picnic is at the end of the minor road in **Glen Etive** (photographs pages 27, 28-29), by the shore of the loch.

6 SANDWICHES ON A THRONE ABOVE ROYALTY

Car tour 5: Park in Craigendarroch Walk, **Ballater** and follow the blue-coded trail beginning at the top of this residential road, signposted 'To Top'. Twisting up through woods on the south side of the hill, it emerges amidst heather and Scots pines at the summit of Craigendarroch in 20-25 minutes (photograph opposite). Ballater is straight below, and the view across Royal Deeside is magnificent. Early morning in summer is the ideal time to catch the light on the craggy face of distant Lochnagar.

7 OSPREY'S-EYE VIEW OF STRATHSPEY

Car tour 6: At the **Revack Estate**, follow the yellow-coded trail from the car park, leading up to the high point above the trees. The foliage is beginning to screen the views, but a fantastic impression of the plains of the Spey Valley, contrasting with the grandeur of the Cairngorm Mountains, is still to be savoured. This easy climb can be made in less than 20 minutes, with even less time needed to return.

Picnic 6 and
Car tour 5:
the summit of
Craigendarroch,
above Ballater

8 IN THE COMPANY OF FIVE SISTERS

Car tour 7: No need to walk anywhere to eat your sandwiches in the **Bealach Ratagan**. Simply park your car and enjoy one of the classic views of the Western Highlands from the car park. The Five Sisters are the range of shapely peaks seen across the head of Loch Duich.

9 OVERLOOKING PLOCKTON

Car tour 7: From the road in **Strathellen Wood above Plockton**, climb to the viewpoint at Creag nan Garadh in less than 15 minutes. This is on NTS land, and the view across the cottage-backed, palm-fringed bay is idyllic — a prospect which extends across Loch Carron and Loch Kishorn to the mountains of Applecross Forest.

10 KILT ROCK

Car tour 8: This break in your journey involves no walking. Just south of Staffin, there are picnic tables at a fabulous viewpoint for the coastal cliffs at **Kilt Rock** (so named because their columns of dolomitic rock have a close resemblance to the pleats of a kilt). A dramatic plunging waterfall is close to the car park, while across the sea there is a fine view of the Torridon mountains on the mainland. Picnic stops almost anywhere else on the **Trotternish Peninsula** or on the **Elgol road** will be equally enjoyable.

11 LUNCH IN THE PRIMEVAL FOREST

Car tour 9: Of the few surviving fragments of the native pine forest of Caledon, the remnant at Coille na Glas Leitire, on the **Beinn Eighe NNR**, is scenically one of the finest. Park in the lochside car park and set off on the waymarked and easy to follow 'Woodland Trail', emerging at the viewpoint plinth after a climb of about 100m/325ft lasting 20 minutes. As you linger among ancient forest pines, looking out across lovely Loch Maree to the primeval bulk of Slioch, you can feel the past. Completing the easy circular trail you are on allows you to return to your car by a different path. Suggesting other picnic spots in this area would be somewhat superfluous; just follow your own instincts and pull over wherever you like.

12 RIVERSIDE PICNIC

Car tour 10: To work up an appetite, walk upstream to the **Falls of Kirkaig** to enjoy your lunch, although this takes nearly an hour each way from Inverkirkaig. For a very lazy time, at a quiet part of the river beneath the roadside trees, simply use the picnic tables in the car park at the bridge over the **River Kirkaig**. In this way, you are free to indulge in a pastime that has become something of a British institution (much to the amusement of foreign visitors): flasks of tea and endless cheese and pickle sandwiches pouring out of the back of the hatchback at the roadside, a real home-from-home.

● Touring

Highlanders will tell you that 'if two sheep can pass each other with room to spare, then the road is quite wide enough'. This says much about rural priorities on the narrow strips of tarmac which dissect Scotland's wild moors and mountains. As you drive along, probably in third gear, dipping and rising and twisting and turning, cattle and sheep can appear suddenly from nowhere! The minor roads of the Highlands will test your driving reactions, and don't expect to average more than about 40km/25mi per hour. In truth you can travel much faster on *some* of the A-roads (although A-road designation is no guarantee of road width).

The first and most important point to bear in mind when driving in the Highlands is that here, as in the rest of Britain, we **drive on the left**. Drivers from abroad, who have spent a lifetime of driving on the right-hand side of the road in their left-hand drive vehicles, tend to forget this simple but vital rule with surprising frequency. Every summer sees the same predictable tally of accidents caused by tourists slipping back to the habits of home, sometimes with fatal results.

One other cause of accidents is that born of frustration where locals, or those with a sense or urgency, caught behind a string of traffic, can seem desperate to overtake. If you notice someone attempting to overtake you, then pull over at the earliest opportunity. It is as well to realise that **it is the custom in Scotland to allow those drivers who obviously want to pass, to pass**.

I have devised ten separate car tours throughout the Highlands. With each one my intention has been to reflect the unique scenic splendours of that particular region, hopefully tempting you to get out and explore a bit more, by **taking you to the starting point of some delightful walks**. The tours are all roughly circular in nature and each begins and ends in the same village or town, your most likely base in that area. If you were to do them all, then I hope you would have gained as comprehensive an overview of the true character of the Scottish Highlands as is possible in about 40 hours of driving.

Because these car tours cover a vast geographical area and are mostly quite detached from one another, they are not easily linked. In any case, it is likely that you will be holidaying in just one or two specific parts of the Highlands on any one visit, where perhaps trying just three or four car tours would be the appropriate approach during your stay.

Wherever I refer to 'minor roads' when describing the car tours, it means a **single-lane road with passing places**. Each passing place is signposted, with the words 'Passing Place' appearing within a white diamond-shaped sign beside the road. They are located at regular intervals along minor roads, allowing vehicles travelling in opposite directions to pass each other or providing you with the opportunity to pull over and allow drivers behind you to overtake. **Passing places are *not* for parking in!** Most roads in the remoter parts of the Highlands, as well as some A-roads, are single-lane, but are never busy. Traffic jams are mostly unheard-of in the Highlands, even on A-roads. None of my suggested tours uses unsurfaced roads or tracks.

Something you will quickly become aware of when driving along the coast roads are the rather odd, large circular and square shapes out in the water. These are the cages of fish farms, mostly salmon cages, now a common feature in just about every sea loch on the west coast. For better or for worse, salmon farming is now a major industry in the Scottish Highlands, apparently to satisfy our demands for cheap fish.

Before heading into the Highlands from the south, as most of you will, **fill your tank to the brim**. Prices in Britain are high as it is (Americans in particular will feel the pinch), but in the Scottish Highlands, fuel is at a premium. And remember that in the remote areas of the north, petrol and diesel will not be available anywhere on Sundays, so keep an eye on your fuel gauge.

The pull-out touring map is designed to be held out opposite the touring notes and contains all the information you will need outside the towns. (As this book is a *countryside guide*, I assume that you will tour with a good standard guide book; historical references in this book are very brief.)

At frequent and appropriate intervals, I have quoted in brackets a *cumulative distance* covered on that particular car tour, in both miles and kilometres (miles are shown first, as all signposting is in miles). The **symbols** used in the touring notes correspond to those on the touring map and are explained on the map key.

1 WILD COUNTRY OF REBELS AND POETS

Callander • Brig o' Turk • Trossachs Pier • Aberfoyle • Inversnaid • Port of Menteith • Callander

93.5km/58mi; about 3 hours' driving

On route: Picnic 1 (see page 11); Walks 1-4

A circular tour through the 'Highlands in miniature' on A-roads with a return trip out to Loch Lomond's 'Bonnie Banks' on a lingering single-track road with passing places. This land of evocative lochs, forests, mountains and glens has been the haunt of both the 'Highland Robin Hood' as well as one of Scotland's most celebrated poets. Easily accessible from the A84, a main trunk road to the Highlands. Spectacularly colourful in autumn.

'So wondrous wild / the whole might seem
The scenery of / a fairy dream.'

Sir Walter Scott's description of The Trossachs, in his 19th-century poem 'The Lady of the Lake', is as apt today as it was then. The experience of beautiful scenery is the great pleasure of this car tour. These landscapes possess a Highland character all their own, being distinctly prettier, less harsh, and on a smaller scale than those encountered further north.

The bustling tourist town of **Callander**★ (*i*✝️♦♦✕🏪 ⊕🚃⛱WC; Walks 1 and 2), with its many hotels and souvenir shops dispensing tartan and shortbread by the bucket-load, is the obvious base from which to explore 'Rob Roy Country'.

Drive west out of Callander on the A84. Just beyond the Woollen Mill at **Kilmahog**★ (1.2mi/2km ✕WC), turn left on the A821, signposted for Aberfoyle. A little further on you can glance across Callander Meadows, back towards the town, before the road comes alongside Loch Venachar. There are numerous lay-bys at gaps in the oaks and alders by the shore of the loch on your left, perfect for picnicking and for admiring Ben Venue from across the water.

Almost hidden by the trees, **Brig o' Turk** (6.5mi/10.5km ♦✕) is an attractive little village with a good tea room/restaurant and the Byre Inn. Thoroughly recommended is a visit to the picturesque Trossachs Kirk (8mi/13km ✝️🚃), idyllically situated close to the loch shore on the left. The key to the church can be obtained locally, or you can simply sit out on the vestry side of the kirk, overlooking **Loch Achray** — a blissful spot, shown in the photograph opposite.

Slate-roofed, with spired turrets, the Victorian Trossachs Hotel (♦♦) exhibits all the features of classic Scottish castle architecture, while immediately west of it

16

lies the wooded country that is the true heart of The Trossachs (Walk 3; with parking at the northwest corner of the loch). A 1.5km side-trip west to the **Trossachs Pier★** (10mi/16km ✕⌖⌂WC) is well worthwhile. If you time your visit right (April to September), you can board the famous steamer, the SS Sir Walter Scott, for a tour of lovely Loch Katrine.

Drive on past the Achray Hotel (11mi/18km ▲✕). As

Ben Venue from Loch Achray

the road bears south and climbs to the **Duke's Pass★** (13.5mi/22km 📷🚌), Loch Achray is left behind. There are car parks and forest drives among the swathes of spruce and fir in Achray Forest, where the Forestry Commission is keen to show off Queen Elizabeth Forest Park at its best. For the definitive view of The Trossachs, wander up to the famous viewpoint, signposted on the right. A view indicator identifies all the main features of the area.

Continue south and, when the road starts to twist downhill, there is a fine view ahead across the lowlands. The FC Visitor Centre (*i*) justifies a stop if you want more information about this area.

Aberfoyle★ (17mi/27km *i*🏨🏕✕🍴⊕🚌WC) is at the bottom of the hill. This is the other main tourist centre of

Top: Ben Ledi from the River Teith at Callander (Walks 1 and 2); middle: Ben Lomond from Loch Ard; bottom: Arrochar Alps from Loch Arklet at Inversnaid (Walk 4)

The Trossachs — a quieter, less frantic alternative to Callander, despite its much-hyped Wool Centre.

Before heading back east towards Callander, take the minor single-lane road signposted 'Inversnaid B829'. It is a delightfully lingering 15mi/24km to the waterfall at **Inversnaid★** (31.5mi/51km ♿🏧🏨▲✕🅿🖼WC), where the road ends at the 'Bonnie Banks' of Loch Lomond. Walk 4, the delightful wildlife ramble illustrated opposite and on page 61, begins at the large public car park by the Inversnaid Hotel at the end of this road. The road skirts the picnic-friendly shores of Lochs Ard, Dhu and Chon. With every mile, the mountain drama intensifies, reaching a stunning climax when the Arrochar Alps come into view across Loch Arklet.

Drive back through **Aberfoyle** (46.5mi/75km). Just over half a mile/1km or so beyond the village, turn left opposite the Rob Roy Motel and follow the A81 towards Callander and Stirling. The road soon comes alongside Scotland's only 'lake', the **Lake of Menteith** (51mi/82km ♿🏨✕🅿🖼WC; photograph page 10) — the spelling error of Dutch cartographers in the 16th century which still stands uncorrected. Turn off right on the B8034 for access to the parking bays along the eastern shore and for the tiny passenger ferry out to **Inchmahome Priory★** (♿🖼WC; Picnic 1). The lake, brimming with trout, is popular with fishermen and ospreys alike.

After driving 1.2mi/2km east of **Port of Menteith**, turn left at the junction with the A873, returning to **Callander** (58mi/93.5km) via the Torrie Forest plantations and the A81.

2 ARGYLL

Tarbet • Arrochar • Inveraray • Lochawe • Dalmally • Bridge of Orchy • Victoria Bridge • Tyndrum • Crianlarich • Tarbet

151km/94mi; about 4 hours' driving (add 18km/11mi; 1 hour for the detour to Lochgoilhead)

On route: Picnic 2 (see pages 11-12); Walks 5, 6, 7

By highland standards the roads on this tour are mostly good and fast, including the A82, one of the busiest roads into the mountains. This circular tour explores the eastern part of Argyll, ideal for those of you holidaying by Loch Lomond or based in the Arrochar, Inveraray, Tyndrum or Crianlarich areas. It is also a very convenient tour if you are visiting Glasgow. Tarbet is just one hour from the city centre by car, which is why I have chosen this village as the start point.

Argyll derives from 'Arag haidal' which means 'Boundary of the Gaels', as it was in this region that the Irish Celts first settled in Scotland in the sixth century, bringing with them Christianity and the Gaelic language. Today, strictly speaking, Argyll is within Strathclyde Region which, both culturally and geographically, means that it is part of a transitional area between highland and lowland. Not surprisingly then, you can expect to enjoy a rich variety of scenery on this car tour — vast sea and inland lochs, lush natural forests and dense plantations, as well as dramatic mountain landscapes.

Leave **Tarbet** (*i*▲▲✕▣♐WC), on the busy west banks of Loch Lomond — the largest area of fresh water in Britain — by heading west on the A83 to **Arrochar** (1.5mi/2.5km ✝▲▲✕♐WC). A short way further along, at **Succoth** (parking for Walk 5), the road curves around the head of the aptly-named sea loch, Loch Long, and into the Argyll Forest Park area. High up in Glen Croe, the plantation conifers give way to open mountain slopes at '**Rest and be Thankful**' (8.5mi/13.5km 📷), a very fine viewpoint. From here an 11mi/18km (return) detour on the B828 and B839 would take you to the charming beauty spot of Lochgoilhead. The main tour continues north and west, to the head of Loch Fyne, another long inlet of the Atlantic. Seafood lovers should visit the Loch Fyne Oysters smokery by **Clachan★** (15.5km/ 25km ✕♐WC). Internationally renowned, their delicious smoked salmon and oysters can be sampled at the adjoining restaurant.

20

Further west, the attractive whitewashed town of **Inveraray**★   (23.5mi/38km   *i*▮✝▮▮▲▲▲✕▱⊕▱▱☂WC) overlooks the bay named Loch Fyne. An exceptional view of the town and the surrounding glens is the reward for a walk up to the folly tower and to Dun na Cuaiche. Inveraray Castle, home of the Duke of Argyll, is open to the public, as is the old Georgian jail.

Leave the capital of Argyll by the A819. Having descended Glen Aray, you will soon reach Loch Awe, the longest stretch of fresh water in Britain. Looming high above the opposite shore, there is no ignoring mighty Ben Cruachan, one of Scotland's finest mountains. Turn left at the A85, to the romantic but crumbling remains of **Kilchurn Castle**★   (39mi/63km   ▮▱; Picnic 2). Further around the loch, just past **Lochawe** (40mi/65km ▲▲✕) is the elaborate and beautiful St Conan's Kirk (✝), the so-called 'show piece of Argyll'. For lovers of church architecture, it is a real treat.

The tranquil B8077 is the more attractive, if less direct, option for driving

Top: Inveraray Castle;
middle: Kilchurn Castle,
Loch Awe (Picnic 2);
bottom: Loch Tulla

View across Strath Fillan, near Tyndrum, to Ben Lui

back east to **Dalmally** (45mi/73km ♦♠♠♠✕ 🚌⊕WC). After a further 2mi/3km along the A85, turn left to join the single-lane B8074 through Glen Orchy, following the most delightful of salmon rivers between confining valley sides. On joining the A82, turn left for **Bridge of Orchy** (57.5mi/93km ♠♠✕🎞WC). From the hotel here, take the minor road to **Inveroran** (61mi/98km ♠♠✕🎞WC), passing through a beautiful remnant of Scots pine forest on your way around to Loch Tulla. Do please heed the warning: 'That which burns never returns'. The road ends at **Victoria Bridge** where Walks 6 and 7 begin, in the vicinity of the spectacular mountains shown on pages 68-69.

Drive back to **Bridge of Orchy** and follow the A82 south to the humdrum tourist village of **Tyndrum**★ (72mi/116km ♠♠♠✕🚌⊕△WC). Further south still, turn right to continue on the A82 from **Crianlarich** (77mi/124km ♠♠♠✕⊕WC). With its cascading river and isolated Scots pines, the drive through Glen Falloch (photograph page 1) is very pleasant, and the Falls of Falloch★ are a popular picnicking area. At **Inverarnan** (83mi/134km ♠✕△WC), you pass the Drovers Inn, the most unusual of pubs — full of stuffed animals, with books and a cosy fireplace. Its bedrooms are said to be visited by ghosts! The viewpoint at **Inveruglas**★ (89mi/143km 🎞🎞WC), back on the banks of Loch Lomond, is another popular picnicking area. In summer a passenger ferry crosses the loch to Inversnaid (Walk 4). From here it is a further 5mi/8km south beside the 'bonnie' west bank to **Tarbet** (94mi/151km).

22

3 BEAUTIFUL TAYSIDE

Killin • Ardeonaig • Kenmore • Fortingall • Bridge of Balgie • Ben Lawers • Glen Lochay • Killin • Glen Dochart • Killin

121km/75mi; about 4 hours' driving (omitting Glen Dochart and Glen Lochay, 79km/49mi; up to 3 hours' driving)

On route: Picnic 3 (see pages 11-12); Walks 8, 9, 10

A drive along the tranquil shores of Loch Tay, past the oldest tree in Europe, and on through 'Scotland's most beautiful glen'. This circuit also begins and ends at the Falls of Dochart, one of the most popular beauty spots in the Highlands.

Loch Tay is not only acknowledged as one of the most delightful lochs in Scotland scenically, but is highly valued by salmon fishermen too. A long and narrow ribbon of inland water, it straddles the land between the austere mountains of the west and the lush, fertile river valleys and plains of Perthshire. One or two notable glens dissect the Breadalbane Mountains; hidden from the main roads and never overcrowded, they remain the undiscovered jewels of Tayside. All this can be seen without moving from your car!

From the spectacular Falls of Dochart, leave **Killin**★ (*i*❚✚🛖🛆✕🅿⊕🚉📷WC; Walk 8) by the minor road signposted 'Loch Tay South'. In summer, visitors arrive by the coach-load to admire these turbulent rapids from the parapet of the picturesque bridge. Backed by the dramatic Tarmachan and Lawers ranges, it is easy to see why so much film gets used up here! Going up through Achmore Woods, there is soon a parking bay on your left, by the loch shore (2mi/3.5km). There are some wonderful views

View from Kenmore across Loch Tay to Ben Lawers

from this undulating minor road, looking across the water to Ben Lawers.

At **Ardeonaig** (7mi/11km ⛺🚻WC), cross the bridge over the Finglen Burn and continue driving higher above the loch shore. Looking in both directions (not the driver!), you can see along almost the entire length of Loch Tay. Further on, at **Acharn**★ (14.5mi/23.5km ⛺🍴WC), the Scottish Crannog Centre (**M**) is well worth a visit — a *crannog* being a solitary dwelling built out on the waters of a loch and connected by a causeway. Nearby is a small fish farm, and among the crafts people based in the hamlet itself is a horn carver who fashions his curious wares from the antlers of local red deer stags.

As you might expect, this east end of Loch Tay is distinctly less mountainous. Attractive **Kenmore**★ (16.5mi/26.5km *i*⛺🍴⛺⛺△🍴🚐🖥WC) is situated at the loch's eastern extremity, its whitewashed houses clustered around the A827 bridge over the River Tay. The village is a lively outdoor pursuits centre specialising, not surprisingly, in sailing, windsurfing and fishing, but also catering for hillwalkers.

From the north side of the village, near the Kenmore Club, take the Tummel Bridge turn-off on the right. Skirting Tayside Forest Park, the road twists north, joining the B846 at the bridge over the River Lyon. Turn left again at **Keltneyburn** (20mi/32km) to reach the picture-postcard village of **Fortingall**★ (22.5mi/36.5km ⛺⛺🍴WC), with its pretty thatched cottages. Of more fame however is the 4000-year-old Fortingall yew tree, reputedly the oldest living thing in Europe!

Just west of Fortingall turn right, signposted for Glen Lyon. This glen is the longest in Scotland and, although constricted by high mountains on both sides, its pastoral

24

Left: Glen Lyon — the tranquil River Lyon weaves its timeless way through trees and lush meadows at Roromore (Walk 9); right: the view west from Ben Lawers (Walk 10)

tranquillity is never threatened. Follow the tree-lined River Lyon upstream, passing open meadows and the occasional croft, as well as a few big houses. There are plenty of reasons to stop the car before reaching the hamlet of **Bridge of Balgie★** (35mi/56.5km ✗☕WC; Walk 9). The main tour leaves this delightful valley by the bridge over the river (although it is possible to drive further west, to its uppermost reaches, at the foot of remote mountain slopes).

From Bridge of Balgie, the tour follows a steep and adventurous single-lane road, climbing the high pass which joins Glen Lyon with Loch Tay. Scenically, it is a rewarding drive, hemmed in between the Ben Lawers and Tarmachan ranges. A roadside cairn (39.5mi/63.5km) marks its highest point at about 500m altitude; winter snows frequently make the road impassable. Beyond Loch na Larige and 1.2mi/2km below the Lawers Dam, you will reach the **NT Visitor Centre on Ben Lawers★** (42mi/68km *i*WC; Picnic 3). A third of the way up a mountain is not the ideal spot for such a building, a blot on the landscape, but the car park does at least provide a significant headstart for Walk 10.

Turn right at the A827, on the north shore of Loch Tay, returning towards Killin. Before driving back through the village however, turn left at the Bridge of Lochay (48mi/77km) and follow a twisting road west beside a river and through intimate **Glen Lochay**, a 16mi/25km return side-trip to the end of the road and back, not to be missed!

On returning to **Killin** again (64mi/103km), I also recommend one more short detour, in Glen Dochart. Follow the minor road beginning just before the bridge at the Falls of Dochart, signposted 'Craignavie Road', along the north side of the River Dochart. In contrast to earlier encounters, **Glen Dochart** (photographs pages 72 and 73) is a much less claustrophobic valley, with mighty Ben More and Stob Binnien dominating the view towards Crianlarich. Cross the bridge at **Ledcharrie** and join the A85, for your third and final return to **Killin** (75mi/121km).

25

4 THE SADDEST GLEN AND THE HIGHEST MOUNTAIN

Fort William • Glen Nevis • Fort William • Onich • Glen Coe • Loch Etive • Glencoe • Kinlochleven • North Ballachulish • Fort William

176km/109.5mi; 4-5 hours' driving (omitting Glen Etive 136km/84.5mi; 3-4 hours' driving or, omitting Glen Nevis, 154km/95.5mi; about 4 hours' driving)

On route: Picnic 4 and Picnic 5 (see pages 11-12); Walks 11-14

This car tour explores the best-known part of the Highlands in the shadow of Ben Nevis, Britain's highest mountain, using the fast A82 as well as quieter minor roads. An obvious base is the thriving tourist town of Fort William, although the villages scattered around the shores of Loch Leven are other popular centres. The scenery of Nether Lochaber has many moods; in places invigorating, in others solemn, but everywhere spectacular.

Sprawling **Fort William**★ (*i*🏃🎿🏛🏨🛖⛺️△✕🛒⊕🚏WC), the capital of the Western Highlands, is no longer a pretty place. With its supermarkets, restaurants and endless choice of accommodation, the town does at least provide for all your practical needs. However, you should not take highland hospitality for granted in Fort William, so be sure to get back into the habit of locking your car!

Within just a few minutes you can be in Glen Nevis, a world away from urban pretensions. Leave the town at the roundabout by the distillery at Nevis Bridge, taking the road signposted '**Glen Nevis**'. Go past the car park at the Visitor Centre on the left and the campsite on the right. The road follows the tree-lined River Nevis upstream past various tourist developments, the last of which is the Youth Hostel (2mi/3.5km; Walk 11; see also photograph page 80). As the road twists south and east between the high mountain ranges of The Mamores on the south side and Ben Nevis on the north side, the skyline is broken by an ever-changing profile of shapely peaks. It was here that Mel Gibson (playing William Wallace), gave

Top: Highland cattle in Glen Nevis; middle: Meall a' Bhuiridh at the top of Glen Etive; bottom: the lower slopes of Ben Nevis from the 'tourist path' (Walk 11)

chase to the English through the reconstructed village in the film 'Braveheart'. Looking to the mountains of Sgurr a' Mhaim and Stob Bàn, perhaps you will recognise the backdrop. On these same meadows, Highland cattle are often to be seen grazing. At **Polldubh**, a popular area with rock climbers, the road crosses the river at the bridge and from here climbs steadily to a car park at the end of the road, where Walk 12 begins and ends (7mi/11km). From here a short walk leads to the beautiful picnic setting shown on page 83, the Steall Waterfall (Picnic 4).

Return to **Fort William** and pick up the A82 going southwest, beside the shores of Loch Linnhe. **Inchree** (23.5mi/38km ▲▲▲△✕WC) is where the ferry connects with Corran. Beyond **Onich** (▲▲) you cross the Ballachulish Bridge (28mi/45km). From the roundabout on the other side, continue on the A82, bypassing the villages of Ballachulish and Glencoe. At the bottom of **Glen Coe** itself, there is a large car park at the **NT Visitor Centre★** (34.5mi/55.5km *i*⌂◉WC), where you can learn about the massacre of 1692, when 38 Macdonalds were slaughtered in their sleep one winter's night by their trusted guests, the Campbells, who at the time were in alliance with the government. Many more perished as they fled into a raging blizzard. Here, in the depths of the 'Glen of Weeping' (*Glen Coe* in Gaelic), the enclosing mountains intensify the atmosphere of solemnity.

Passing Loch Achtriochtan, the drama of high mountains and cliffs on both sides is quite overwhelming, some would say intimidating. Yet this is Scotland's premiere walking and climbing area, and the mountains themselves are exceptionally beautiful, if sometimes threatening. There are car parks further up which give access to exceptional viewpoints and very fine walks (Walk 13). Here, in summer, tartan-clad pipers (photograph page 2) subject visitors to the drone of bagpipes, once a battlefield instrument, but today better heard from three glens away!

In the **Pass of Glencoe** sheer outcrops of rock abut the tarmac abruptly, constricting the road

through a very narrow passage. The road then climbs higher still, finally escaping the confines of the lower glen. The short walk leading to Picnic 5 climbs the 'Devil's Staircase' from **Altnafeadh**. Some 2mi/3km further on, turn right on a minor road signposted 'Glen Etive' (43mi/69km). Cross the River Coupall below the gigantic pyramidal monolith that is Stob Dearg, part of the Buachaille Etive Mòr and possibly the most photographed peak in Scotland, then continue southwest through charming and tranquil **Glen Etive**. The road ends at the sea, at **Loch Etive** (55mi/89km), another setting for Picnic 5.

From here return the same way and rejoin the A82. Turn left and drive back down Glen Coe, possibly even more impressive in this direction. Before reaching the Visitor Centre again, take the old glen road off to the right, past the Clachaig Inn (76mi/123km ▲▲▲✕WC). This delightful unfrequented lane through the trees (∆) crosses the Bridge of Coe (Walk 14) and leads to the village of **Glencoe★** (77.5mi/125km ♨▲▲▲✕☐WC). Where the three roads intersect, turn right and follow the B863 to **Kinlochleven★** (86mi/139km ♨▲▲▲✕☐⊕WC) and then head back west, along the north shore of Loch Leven (photograph pages 86-87). You will regain the A82 at **North Ballachulish** (96mi/154.5km ▲▲▲✕WC) for the return to **Fort William** (109.5mi/176km).

The Buachaille Etive Mòr from the River Etive, Glen Etive

5 ROYAL DEESIDE

Braemar • Balmoral • Bridge of Muick • Glen Muick • Ballater • Balmoral • Braemar • Linn of Dee and Linn of Quoich • Braemar

112.5km/70mi; about 3 hours' driving

On route: Picnic 6 (see pages 11-12); Walks 15-17

The beauty of this area is not typified by high dramatic mountains or lonely, desolate glens. Essentially, Deeside is a long river valley carpeted with vast tracts of Scots pines and dotted with villages and castles. Deeside has been the preferred summer residence of Royals since Queen Victoria first arrived at Balmoral 150 years ago. This car tour follows in the tracks of kings and queens, along the banks of one of Scotland's loveliest rivers.

The scenery of Royal Deeside is as picturesque as any in Scotland and, in contrast to the wild mountain areas of the north and west Highlands, Deeside has a gentle, more welcoming character. The tourist centres of Ballater and Braemar provide all the facilities for a base in Deeside and, while you might set out on this car tour from either village, I have described the route from Braemar.

Braemar★ (*i*♜✝⛰▲✕⛽⊕WC; Walk 15) is probably best known for hosting the most famous Highland Games of them all, the Braemar Gathering, held annually on the first Saturday of September. This is the one the Queen attends, with all available accommodation booked months in advance and the village bursting at the seams, so you might want to avoid the place then.

Leaving the village, head towards Balmoral on the A93, passing Braemar Castle before coming alongside the beautiful banks of the River Dee. Cross the river at the Bridge of Dee (3mi/4.5km). The old Invercauld Bridge can be seen on your right; you might wish to stop and walk out to it. The mature stands of Scots pines on the south side of the river are very extensive, with those at Ballochbuie Forest representing one of the finest

The Braemar Gathering, 1998: start of the fell race up Morrone and (opposite) caber-tossing in front of the Queen and Queen Mother.

examples of native Caledonian Forest in Scotland. There are plenty of good tracks and paths for exploring the unique woods near Balmoral, encountering its rare fauna or perhaps crossing paths with Prince Charles.

Looking across Balmoral Forest from the road, you can glimpse the high flat tableland of the White Mounth plateau, the dramatic highlight of which, in a land that lacks obvious drama, is Lochnagar (Walk 16; photograph page 91). Screened by the trees across the river is Balmoral Castle . Turn right at **Crathie** (9mi/14.5km ♣⛪WC), signposted 'Balmoral and South Deeside' and drive over the bridge, turning sharp left at the entrance to **Balmoral Castle**★ (■⛺⛽; open to the public in May, June and July only). A very pleasant woodland drive follows, along the quiet B976 road and the south bank of the river. You can visit the Royal Lochanagar Distillery on your way to **Bridge of Muick** (16.5mi/26.5km). Here, turn right and go up the minor road through **Glen Muick**, past attractive waterfalls, to the end of the road, where Walk 16 begins and ends at the Spittal of Glenmuick (24.5mi/39.5 km ⊓).

Rejoin the B976 back at Bridge of Muick (32mi/52km) and drive north a little way, to cross the bridge on the left, leading into the neat and tidy village of **Ballater**★ (*i*♣▲▲ ▲△✕➡⊕WC). Ballater folk hold a deep respect for the patronage of Royals, possibly more than a history of serfdom deserves. The village is, undeniably, very attractive. Drive west from here on the main road, passing below the hill at **Craigendarroch** (33.5mi/54km; Picnic 6; photograph page 13). From **Crathie** (40mi/64.5km), continue back along the A93 to **Braemar** (49mi/79km).

Now head west for the Linn of Dee on a glorious little road through the upper reaches of the Dee Valley. The **Linn of Dee** (55.5mi/89.5km) is a popular picnic spot, where the Dee cascades through a pine-fringed channel and under the arch of a stone bridge. Continue beyond Mar Lodge to the **Linn of Quoich** (60mi/97km), another fine picnic spot. From **Allanaquoich**, at the end of the road, a short walk leads out to a footbridge over Quoich Water (Walk 17; photograph pages 94-95).

Return the same way to **Braemar** (70mi/112.5km).

31

6 MONUMENTAL MOUNTAINS AND SKI RUNS, BIG RIVERS AND WHISKY GALORE!

Aviemore • Carrbridge • Grantown-on-Spey • Marypark • Nethy Bridge • Glen More • Glen Feshie • Aviemore

154 km/96 mi; 3-4 hours' driving (omitting Glen Feshie and Loch Inch, 124km/77mi; somewhat over 3 hours' driving)

On route: Picnic 7 (see pages 11-12); Walks 18-20

This car tour ventures along Strathspey in the shadow of the Cairngorms, the highest land mass in Scotland, and Britain's premier ski resort. Good roads run up and down both sides of the River Spey, giving motorists the opportunity to explore the tremendous mountains, rivers and natural forests of the area, with the treat of a 'wee dram' in the distillery of your choice on the Malt Whisky Trail.

Few other areas in the Scottish Highlands can combine so well a variety of different landscapes with the potential for exercising such a diverse range of recreational activities. In the Cairngorms and on Speyside, walkers and climbers, picnickers, skiers, snowboarders, bird-wachers, golfers, clay pigeon-shooters, anglers, off-road drivers, sightseers, canoeists, sailors, artists and malt whisky enthusiasts will all find plenty in which to delight.

Aviemore★ (*i* 🏠 ▲ △ ✕ 🖳 ⊕ 🚗 WC) is the obvious base from which to explore the Cairngorms. The village easily justifies its reputation as an ugly concrete sprawl, but it has all the facilities you could need, providing them on a year-round basis. From Aviemore drive north to gain the A95 (2mi/3.2km) and then join the B9153 to **Carrbridge★** (7mi/11km *i* 🏠 ▲ ✕ 🖳 WC). Turn right on the A938, driving east across a landscape of fertile fields, woods and flat meadows with impressive views south to the Cairngorm Mountains.

At **Dulnain Bridge** (13.5mi/22km ▲ 🖳) you will come alongside the River Dulnain. Here turn left, rejoining the A95 briefly, to pass through **Grantown-on-Spey★**

Glen Feshie: the River Feshie

(16.5mi/26.5km *i* ▲▲ ▲ △ ✗ ▣ ⊕ ☷ WC), a small Georgian town well worth exploring. From here take the B9102, signposted 'Archiestown', driving past the golf club, with its fairways among the pines. Further east, the road climbs above the north bank of the beautiful River Spey, the finest of salmon rivers. Watch out for pheasants on the road! There are plenty of opportunities to pull over, to picnic or to admire the lichen-encrusted larch and birch trees, as well as the views across the valley. There is a car park (24mi/39km ▣) at a particularly good viewpoint.

At **Marypark** turn right on the B9138 (30mi/48.5km) and cross the bridge. Turn left at the A95, if you want to visit one of the many distilleries in the area. Otherwise turn right and continue the tour by heading back down the south bank of the Spey. On crossing the River Avon at **Ballindalloch** (33.5mi/54km ▣), you will notice in the trees a very Scottish-style Victorian bridge and turreted house. Also evident are signs for the Speyside Way, one of Scotland's four long-distance footpaths.

Drive past the Tormore Distillery and go through **Cromdale** (43mi/69km ▲▲ ✗ WC), later rejoining the B970. The **Revack Estate★** has gardens and forest trails to explore (46.5mi/75km ✗ ☷ ❀ ▣ WC; Picnic 7). Beyond **Nethy Bridge**, bird-watchers might like to take a detour to Boat of Garten (0.7mi/1.2km; signposted to the right). For guaranteed sightings of ospreys at their famous nest site, visit between April and July. Heading south from here, the Cairngorms massif appears ever closer.

Turn left at **Coylumbridge** (60.5mi/98km ▲▲ △; Walk 18) and follow the Glen More road through the pines of **Glen More** Forest (Walk 19) and along the shores of Loch Morlich, passing exceptionally fine spots for roadside picnics. The ski centre on **Cairn Gorm★** lies at the top of the road (69mi/111km ✦ ✗ ☷ ▣ WC; Walk 20; photographs pages 103-105), its pistes scarring the mountain.

From Cairn Gorm, go back through **Coylumbridge** (75.5mi/122km). Just before Aviemore, turn left on the B970, again following the Spey, to reach **Feshiebridge**. After crossing the River Feshie, take the **Glen Feshie** road from Inch House (84mi/135km). On reaching the river after just 2mi/3km, a locked gate prevents further travel up the glen, but this is a lovely spot, below the wooded slopes at the western edge of the Cairngorm plateau.

Back at Inch House, follow the road to the right, to **Kincraig** and the bird reserve at the top of Loch Inch. Then return to **Aviemore** by the B9152 (96mi/154km).

Plockton • Kyle of Lochalsh • Dornie • Shiel Bridge • Glenelg • Arnisdale • Shiel Bridge • Cluanie Inn • Auchtertyre • Plockton

190km/118 mi; up to 4.5 hours' driving (allow an extra 30 minutes for the detour to the head of Loch Long near the end of the tour)

On route: Picnics 8 and 9 (see pages 11 and 13); Walks 21, 22

Driving on a combination of fast A-roads and remote minor roads, you can explore the stunning scenery around the shores of some of the coastal lochs of the Western Highlands. Some sea-water channels penetrate far inland, while others are very definitely at the edge of the ocean. On this tour, you will also encounter spectacular mountains and glens, Iron Age remains and picturesque castles and villages.

Lochalsh district, together with Glen Shiel, represents the gateway to the Northwest Highlands. Many motorists rush through on the A87, single-mindedly focused on destinations on the Isle of Skye or in Wester Ross or Sutherland. However, the area's many attributes demand that it be explored for itself and savoured. Among the delights to be discovered is a castle that has become one of the Highland's great tourist attractions, a village as pretty as you could imagine anywhere, and a glen that rivals the finest in the country for scenic beauty.

Although not as bustling a centre of activity as Kyle of Lochalsh, **Plockton★** (🏔▲△✕🖼WC) is a quieter and by far more preferable base. Essentially a long line of picturesque cottages strung out around a sheltered bay where palms flourish, it is difficult to disagree with those who assert that Plockton is the prettiest of Scotland's west coast villages. Drive up from the harbour to the bridge at **Duirinish** (2mi/3km). There turn right and follow signs along the minor roads to **Kyle of Lochalsh** (6mi/9.5km 🏔▲✕🚽⊕🖼WC), notable only as the main crossing

Distant mountains of Skye, from Loch Hourn at Arnisdale (Walk 22)

Eilean Donan Castle, Loch Duich

place for the Island of Skye. A bridge rather than a ferry now links the island to the mainland. Not only is it the most expensive toll bridge in the world but, considered purely on environmental grounds, it is an outrage and should never have been built.

Turn left at the A87, signposted for Fort William, following the road beside Loch Alsh and passing the **Balmacara Estate** (9mi/14.5km △❀), before crossing Loch Long at **Dornie★** (14.5mi/23.5km ▲△✕WC). Everyone stops a little further on, at **Eilean Donan Castle** on the shore of Loch Duich (▮; photograph above); you can visit it now or on your return. But *before* reaching the castle, take the old road out of Dornie, signposted 'Carr Brae viewpoint'. It climbs steeply above the shore of Loch Long to a viewpoint at the highest point in the road (16.5mi/27km 📷). From here continue down the old road, to rejoin the A87. Curving around the bay at the head of the Loch Duich, take the road on the left for 'Morvich', continuing along a tarmac track in Strath Croe to the parking place at the **Kintail Country Park** (23mi/37km ⊓; Walk 21). Return to the main road and continue driving south.

At **Shiel Bridge** (27mi/44km ▲△✕🖥) turn right on the minor road that climbs steeply to a famous viewpoint for the Five Sisters of Kintail, at the **Bealach Ratagan** (📷; Picnic 8). Legend has it that the Five Sisters are the five unclaimed daughters of a local farmer, each one transformed by a local wizard into the peaks we see today, so as to preserve their beauty. Only the five brothers promised to them by a visiting family can unlock the spell.

Beyond the *bealach,* the road descends through lush Glen More to the village of **Glenelg** (37mi/60km ▲▲▲ ✕⊓WC). The ferry to Skye is along the little road going northwest from here. Glenelg has a prominent war memorial by the shore, overlooking Glenelg Bay.

Before continuing much further south along the road, the tour heads east briefly from the hamlet of Eilanreach, to the Brochs of Gleann Beag. Among them is Dun Telve, one of the best preserved of the hundreds of *brochs*

Loch Hourn from the Arnisdale road, below Beinn Sgritheall (Walk 22)

(circular stone towers) in Scotland; they were built as defences against Viking invaders. Also worth viewing is the waterfall in Gleann Beag.

Drive back to the bridge near the mouth of the Abhainn à Ghlinne Bhig (45mi/72.5km), then turn left and follow the magnificent coastal road to Loch Hourn. Walk 22 begins and ends in the hamlet of **Arnisdale** (54mi/87km), a spectacularly remote setting. Remote it may be, but you will find refreshments at Sheena's Tea Hut. The road ends some 0.6mi/1km further on, at Corran.

Drive back to **Shiel Bridge** (75mi/121km), turn right at the A87 and follow the fast road through Glen Shiel to **Cluanie Inn** (86.5mi/139.5km ▲✕🖻WC). Hemmed in by lofty mountain ranges, the glen is not oppressive in the way that Glen Coe can be; scenes of exceptional beauty abound, with plenty to occupy Munroists. Walking the roller-coaster ridge linking the shapely peaks of the Five Sisters is a formidable but popular challenge.

Drive back from Cluanie Inn along the A87 as far as **Dornie**, but not before being distracted, along with everyone else, by Eilean Donan Castle. Having been used as a location to sell everything from shortbread to cars, it is the most photographed castle in the Highlands. Just after crossing Loch Long again, you may like to turn right on a minor road to the head of the loch — a lovely little detour. At **Auchtertyre** (108mi/174km) turn right on the A890. After a further 3.5mi/5.5km, take the minor road off left for Plockton. The road, below the cliffs of Creag an Duilisg, skirts the shore of Loch Carron and then rises through Strathellen Wood (Picnic 9), before finally descending to **Plockton** (118mi/190km).

8 THE ISLAND OF MIST

Portree • Staffin • Uig • Portree • Sligachan • Broadford • Elgol • Portree

213km/133mi; about 5 hours' driving (the northern stretch is 87km/54mi; 2 hours, and the southern stretch 127km/79mi; 3 hours)

On route: Picnic 10 (see pages 11 and 13); Walks 23-25

With its magnificent Cuillin range, the Isle of Skye boasts the finest mountain scenery in the British Isles. The island is adorned with many other unusual land forms, with countless attractions for non-walkers too. By good fortune, Skye is readily accessible from the mainland. Using mostly excellent A-roads, this car tour visits the very best of the island. Since it describes a figure of eight, it is a tour easily split into two parts, thus giving you the option of two days of easy driving.

Since the opening of the highly-controversial road bridge in 1995, the Isle of Skye is technically no longer an island. For toll-paying motorists it is the most expensive bridge in the world; in the opinion of almost everyone else, it is the environmental cost that has been so difficult to swallow. A more romantic (and politically correct) crossing can still be made using the tiny Kylerhea Ferry (6 cars at a time) from Glenelg which, perhaps as a symbolic act of defiance, is 10p cheaper than the bridge.

Skye is the most popular of all the Scottish islands, partly because it is so easily accessible, but principally because of its magnificent scenery and excellent tourist facilities. But be warned, it is not without good reason that the Gaelic name for Skye, *Eilean à Cheo*, means 'Island of Mist'.

Portree is the attractive capital town of Skye, a perfect place to stay and from which to tour. If you are travelling from the south, having just crossed from the mainland, it would be easy to complete the southern section of this tour on your way up. Otherwise, you can explore the Trotternish Peninsula first.

From **Portree★** (*i* ▲▲ ▲ △ ✕ ♟ ⊕ ☰ WC) drive north on the A855, passing Loch Fada and Loch Leathan and then a parking place by the plantation on your left (7mi/11.5km), where Walk 23 begins and ends (photograph page 112). The road follows the length of the Trotternish Ridge from here on, soon coming close to the coast and passing a fine viewpoint on the right (10mi/16.5km ☰ ☏). You can investigate further on foot by a path which ventures along this marvellous bit of rocky coastline.

The waterfall and little gorge at Inver Tote is worth stopping for, as is the popular signposted viewpoint for **Kilt Rock** (16mi/25.5km ☰ ☏ WC; Picnic 10). Across the sea, the Torridon Mountains (Car tour 9) on the mainland

Bla Bheinn, from across Loch Slapin at Torrin

are well seen from here. At **Brogaig** (19mi/31km WC), just inland from Staffin Bay, take the minor road on the left for a short side-trip to the higher of two car parks (21mi/34km; Walk 24), enjoying breathtaking views along the Trotternish Ridge, to the remarkable rock formations at the Quiraing (📷; photograph page 115). Then drive back down to the main road at **Brogaig** and continue north.

The road turns west around the top of the peninsula, giving excellent views to the Western Isles. You can stroll out to the ruins of **Duntulm Castle★** (30.5mi/49km ▥ ▲▲📷), which claims to be the home of piping, before turning south down the west coast. After another 2mi/3km, you will pass a hamlet of restored blackhouses (**M**; traditional thatched cottages of the Hebrides) near the burial place of Flora MacDonald, the Jacobite heroine of Skye. Having driven across a flatter landscape scattered with crofts, the road descends sharply to **Uig★** (38.5mi/62km ▲▲▲△✕🖳WC), from where the Outer Isles ferry sails. Further south on the A87, you reach the junction with the A850 at **Borve** (50mi/80.5km 🖳WC), before returning to **Portree** (53.5mi/86km).

To continue the tour, turn right along the A87. Through the forestry plantations in Glen Varragill the view ahead is dominated by the magnificent mountains of the Cuillin. The much-photographed view of their sharp and shattered peaks shown on pages 116-117 was taken from the old bridge at **Sligachan** (63mi/101km ▲▲✕△📷WC), where Walk 25 ends. From here the road follows the shore of Loch Sligachan and the coast, to the large village of **Broadford★** (79mi/127km *i*▲▲▲✕🖳⊕🎋WC). Turn right here on the B8083, passing the marble quarry at **Torrin** and then rounding the head of beautiful Loch Slapin. The huge jagged mass of gabbro rock rising above the water is Bla Bheinn, undoubtedly one of the finest mountains on Skye. The road comes to an end at **Elgol** (93mi/150km ▲✕📷WC), the starting-point for Walk 25. From the jetty here, you can savour the spectacular serrated skyline of the Cuillin peaks across Loch Scavaig in what is, for many, the finest coastal view in the British Isles.

Take the same roads back to **Portree** (133mi/213km).

9 TORRIDON AND APPLECROSS

Kinlochewe • Torridon • Lower Diabaig • Shieldaig • Applecross • Bealach na Bà • Lochcarron • Achnasheen • Kinlochewe • Beinn Eighe NNR • Kinlochewe

187km/116mi; about 4 hours' driving (avoiding the detour to Diabaig: 159km/99mi; about 3.5 hours' driving, or, bypassing the Applecross peninsula by remaining on the A896 between Shieldaig and Loch Carron: 143km/89mi; about 3 hours' driving)

On route: Picnic 11 (see pages 11 and 13); Walks 26-28

This circuit explores Glen Torridon, Glen Carron and the Applecross peninsula. You will follow A-roads for about half the total distance although, perhaps here more than anywhere else, this is no guarantee of driving for very long in top gear! Without even leaving your car you will come close to mountains of immense rugged grandeur, the 'scenic gems' of Torridon — very easy to survey from roadside viewpoints. Another 'high point' of this tour is the pass at 628m/2060ft!

Wester Ross claims some of the wildest countryside in Europe. With extensive outcrops of Lewisian gneiss over 2.7 billion years old, the region also boasts some of the oldest rocks on the entire planet, while some of Scotland's most striking mountains have been carved from Torridon sandstone formed 800 million years ago. Such timescales are difficult to comprehend, but consider that by comparison, you and I are here and gone in the blink of a geological eye. Yet so evocative of prehistory is this untamed landscape that you would swear you could see dinosaurs tracking across the moor! While the Torridons are often referred to as the 'scenic gems' of Wester Ross, I have my own good reasons why Torridon can never be ignored: among mountains, they are my favourite in all Scotland.

Start the tour from **Kinlochewe** (*i* 🏔🏔🏔△✕🖥WC) which, although not the largest village visited on this tour,

Loch Shieldaig

is strategically the most important settlement. Take the A896 signposted 'Torridon' and 'Shieldaig', passing below Beinn Eighe at the edge of the NNR. Beinn Eighe is an assemblage of peaks joined by a long quartzite scree-covered ridge and therefore looks more like a mountain range than a single mountain. It is seen to best effect across the waters of Loch Clair and Loch Coulin, both of which are accessible on foot along the private road on your left (3mi/5km). The other huge mass which dominates Glen Torridon on its northern flank is mighty Liathach. As you come below this sandstone giant, the main glen car park, base for Walk 26, is on your right (6mi/10km).

Take the minor road off to the right at the **Torridon Countryside Centre**★ (10mi/16km *i*△WC), passing through **Torridon** village (10.5mi/17km ♠) on the glorious little road above the northern shore of Upper Loch Torridon. Go all the way to the end, to the picturesque village of **Lower Diabaig** (18.5mi/30km ♠), skirting below the most westerly of the Torridonian triptych of mountains, Beinn Alligin. It is well worth stopping to view the waterfalls in the Coire Mhic Nòbuil (starting point for Walk 27), as well as the quaint Torridon kirk (⚜) nearby, before returning to rejoin the A896 (27mi/44km).

Turn right and follow the road above the southern shore of the loch, passing through **Annat**. You should take a break at the Torridon Hotel (29mi/46.5km ♠♠✕⊇WC), just for the special treat of coffee in a plush Scottish countryhouse setting, with a great view from the window. The road then climbs to a popular viewpoint (30.5mi/49km 📷) overlooking the loch and taking in the commanding grandeur of both Beinn Alligin and Liathach.

View across Upper Loch Torridon from the A896 near Shieldaig

Upper Loch Torridon from near Diabaig

At **Shieldaig** (34mi/55km ⛰️⛰️ ▲ ✕ WC), turn right to have a look at the village, rejoining the main road at the far end. Turn right for 'Applecross' and 'Kenmore', continuing around the pine-fringed bay of Loch Shieldaig on a minor road which offers glorious views across Loch Torridon. Soon after bypassing the hamlet of Kenmore (42mi/68km), bear left and follow the coastal road south. From here you will enjoy prolonged views to the islands of Rona, Raasay and Skye, across the Inner Sound. Pull over in any one of a number of car parks before eventually turning into the village of **Applecross** (57mi/92km ⛰️⛰️ ▲ △ ✕ 🅿️ WC).

From Applecross take the road which rises steadily up over the moor to the large car park at the top of the **Bealach na Bà** (62.5mi/100.5km 📷). At 628m/2060ft, this is possibly the finest vantage point from a car seat anywhere in Scotland. The views to Skye on a clear day are breathtaking, as is the drama of the *bealach* itself.

Begin the tortuous descent towards Loch Kishorn via a series of sharp hairpins, an experience that will test the nerves of timid drivers. On reaching the River Kishorn (70.5mi/114km), turn right, rejoining the A896 and soon arriving at the village of **Lochcarron★** (77mi/124km ⛰️⛰️ ▲ ✕ 🅿️ WC). At the next junction (80mi/129km), continue through Glen Carron on the A890. Go past **Achnashellach** (85.5mi/138km), the base for Walk 28, which explores the magnificent setting shown on page 127. At the top of the glen, at **Achnasheen** (98mi/158km ⛰️⛰️ ▲ ✕ 🅿️ WC), turn left for 'Kinlochewe' and drive along the single-lane A832, descending Glen Docherty towards lovely Loch Maree at the bottom.

Having returned to **Kinlochewe** (107mi/172km), continue a little further along the A832, to explore the beautiful Scots pines of the NNR, the forested face of **Beinn Eighe** (Picnic 11). The giant molar tooth of a mountain, Slioch, is seen to best effect across Loch Maree from the parking bay 2mi/3km beyond the 'Trail' car park. Return to **Kinlochewe** again the same way (116mi/187km).

10 ASSYNT AND COIGACH

Lochinver • Stoer • Drumbeg • Inchnadamph • Knockan • Drumrunie • Lochinver

106km/65mi; 2.5 to 3 hours' driving. (The A837 between Lochinver and the Skiag Bridge at Loch Assynt allows this car tour to be split into two parts: northern coastal section of 61km/38mi; up to 1.5 hours' driving, or the southern section circling Inverpolly NNR — 76km/47mi; up to 2 hours' driving.)

On route: Picnic 12 (see pages 11 and 13); Walks 29, 30

This circuit follows unfrequented minor roads to explore a wonderful coastline on the far northwest edge of the Scottish mainland. Much faster A-roads allow you to drive unhindered through a landscape of extra-ordinary mountain features. Whether on wheels or on foot in this part of the Scottish Highlands, you are more likely to find solitude than just about anywhere else in Europe.

Much of desolate Sutherland is dominated by vast tracts of wet moorland with outcrops of gnarled grey rock poking through. However, the districts of Assynt and Coigach, straddling the old counties of Sutherland and Wester Ross, are characterised by weird and isolated mountains of Torridonian sandstone. Their forms rise boldly above the *lochan*-studded moors, presenting the most unusual of shapes. Such topographical oddities are part of a landscape that is considered internationally important among geologists, but one which is equally intriguing for sightseers. For variation, this tour also explores the wild and picturesque coastline along the western and northern edges of Assynt.

Lochinver★ (🏨🏪▲✕🛒⊕wc; Walk 29) is the main village of Assynt. Considering its modest size, this would be surprising anywhere else but here in Sutherland — Scotland's least densely-populated county. The village is a popular centre for visiting walkers, climbers and anglers and also a most convenient base for those touring by car.

Follow the A837 north and then, after 1mi/1.5 km, turn left on the B869. If you fancy visiting a sandy bay, then take a detour out to Achmelvich. Otherwise, wait until reaching **Stoer** (6.5mi/10.5km ▲△), where there are other equally fine beaches. Progress is slow on this road across country which nature has left untidy and haphazard, but every mile of it is a delight. Another worthwhile detour is out to the lighthouse at the end of the road at Rubha Stoer. From there you could walk out to a dramatic sea stack, the Old Man of Stoer.

From the sands at **Clashnessie Bay** (8.5mi/13.5km) the road bears east, a journey of ups and downs and twists and turns. There is a very fine viewpoint at **Drumbeg** (13.5mi/22km 🏨▲✕🛒wc), where you can park off the

42

road and look out and across Eddrachillis Bay, a seascape dotted with islands including Handa (RSPB Reserve).

Between the hamlet of **Nedd** and the main road, you will be driving through one or two wooded valleys, delightful green oases between the tracts of barren moor. The coastline is blemished only by the cages of salmon farms, which some people would claim to be necessary environmental anomalies in the name of aquaculture. As well as these modern developments, traditional fishing and crofting activities are still vital to the local economy. It is worth noting that in 1992 the Assynt crofters were successful in bringing the North Assynt Estate into community control, thus ending hundreds of years of ownership by distant landlords. This historic achievement might well prove to be the long overdue turning point in the troubled and tragic history of land ownership in Scotland.

Turn right at the A894 (22.5mi/36.5km), passing between the mountains of Quinag and Glas Bheinn, to reach the shore of Loch Assynt at the A837 (28mi/45km). Continue along the east shore of this loch, passing the crumbling remains of Ardvreck Castle (■). **Inchnadamph Lodge★** (30mi/48km ▲▲ ✕WC) is the base for geological expeditions and walks which explore the unique limestone caves and cliffs of the area.

Leave the A837 for the A835 at **Ledmore** (35.5mi/ 57km). The fascinating geology and wildlife habitats of Inverpolly NNR are of international significance. You can discover more at the Visitor Centre (*i*) below the **Knockan** Cliffs. An easy walk follows the geological trail, where study of the rock exposures here have played an important part in increasing our understanding of the evolution of the earth.

At **Drumrunie** (44.5mi/72.5km), turn right off the A835, signposted 'Achiltibuie 15' and follow this much slower road west. The rugged face of Ben Mór Coigach is seen on your left, across Loch Lurgainn. The path up to an especially sharp and isolated wedge of sandstone, Stac Pollaich, begins from the northern shore of the loch (49mi/79km; Walk 30).

From the west end of Loch Bad a' Ghaill (53mi/ 85.5km), turn right for 'Lochinver 12'. This narrow strip of tarmac threads a way through a tangled landscape of gneiss outcrops, trout filled *lochans*, peat bogs and clumps of woodland, a tortuous but exquisitely beautiful finale to our journey around Assynt and Coigach.

Having reached the coast at Loch an Eisg-brachaidh, cut back inland to cross the River Kirkaig at **Inverkirkaig★** (61.5mi/99km 🏛). Here, you re-enter the old county of Sutherland from Wester Ross (both are now absorbed into the new Highland Region). You can park here and walk up to the lovely Falls of Kirkaig, 2mi/3km upstream (Picnic 12). More surprising, however, is the discovery of Achins Bookshop (reputedly Britain's remotest bookshop), partly screened by the trees just east of the bridge and offering books for sale in defiance, or so it would seem, of any obvious customer base.

From the beautiful bay of Loch Kirkaig, turn northwards back to **Lochinver** (65mi/106km).

The wild wet moor of Sutherland

● *Walking* _____

The Scottish mountains are mere dwarfs compared to the high peaks of the other major mountain ranges of Europe. But despite their modest stature, the virtual absence of clear waymarked footpaths means often rough traverses across untamed countryside, a wilderness lashed by some of the most unpredictable weather on the planet. Consequently, the potential challenge for walkers in the Scottish Highlands can be equal to that presented by far loftier mountains.

Many great explorers and mountaineers have used Scotland as their training ground. Whilst the Scottish mountains demand respect and should never be underestimated, there is a great deal to be enjoyed by those of us who have no aspirations to be pioneers but who wish simply to enjoy the great beauty and variety of landscape and nature.

The walks in this book offer something to suit all abilities and inclinations, from sedate lochside strolls to energetic mountain climbs. There are walks for those seeking grand views, or routes for those more interested in history, wildlife or geology — and there is plenty to keep photographers and artists inspired.

Weather

It is often said that whereas other countries have climate, Scotland has weather. The main feature of Highland weather is changeability. Highlanders will say to you that 'if you do not like a particular season, wait an hour and another will come along'. Indeed, when climbing in the hills, it is not unusual to feel that you have experienced all four seasons in a single day!

The Scottish Highlands have higher rainfall levels than most of the United Kingdom. However, precipitation levels can vary greatly across the region. Weather systems arrive predominantly from the Atlantic, which means that the Western Highlands receive over twice the amount of precipitation as the Cairngorms to the east. This climatic divide results in a more 'continental' effect on the east side, where summers are warmer and winters colder than in the west. Being subject to more frosts and snow than elsewhere, the Cairngorms are renowned for skiing.

45

Scottish weather is notoriously unpredictable but, on balance, the longest spells of dry and settled weather usually occur in the months of May and September.

Safety and equipment

Even the very strenuous walks in this book should not present any great difficulty to experienced walkers. If you are less experienced, then you can work your way up to the tougher routes. However, the Scottish mountains in winter are normally far more serious undertakings than they are in late spring, summer or early autumn. If you are new to the Highlands, then it is advisable to avoid the mountain walks between the end of October and early April, or whenever there is significant snow. At this time, they are mostly the preserve of properly-equipped mountaineers. Such routes might then also become roped expeditions with an array of additional problems and dangers, not least that of having fewer daylight hours to complete a walk.

Three- or four-season walking boots are advisable on all but the easiest walks — those on dry level tracks. At the start of each walk, I have briefly outlined the equipment required. For climbing up to any of the mountain summits in summer, the contents of your rucksack should include the following *as a minimum:*

  waterproof bag liner (a dustbin liner is ideal)
  breathable waterproof outershell (cagoule and trousers)
  map
  compass
  whistle
  adequate food and plenty of liquid
  spare socks
  basic first-aid kit
  warm hat and sunhat
  suncream

At most other times, and certainly in winter, you should add to this list: thermal underwear, emergency food rations, crampons, ice axe, a 'bivvy' bag, head-torch and ski goggles or sunglasses.

Country code

Always respect the **Country code**, wherever you are in the United Kingdom:
- Enjoy the countryside and respect its life and work.
- Guard against all risk of fire.
- Fasten all gates.

- Keep your dogs under close control.
- Keep to public paths across farm land.
- Use gates and stiles to cross fences, hedges and walls.
- Leave livestock, crops and machinery alone.
- Take your litter home.
- Help to keep all water clean.
- Protect wildlife, plants and trees.
- Take special care on country roads.
- Make no unnecessary noise.

If you have a go at any of the walks on the high mountains, be sure also to observe the **Mountain code for Scotland**, as published with relevant OS maps:

Before you go
- Learn the use of map and compass.
- Know the weather signs and local forecast.
- Plan within your capabilities.
- Know simple first-aid and the symptoms of exposure.
- Know the mountain distress signals (see below).
- Know the Country code (see above).

When you go
- If possible, avoid going alone.
- Leave written word of your route and report your return.
- Take windproofs, waterproofs, woollens and survival bag.
- Take map, compass, whistle, torch and food.
- Wear climbing boots.
- Keep alert all day.

If there is snow on the hills
- Always have an ice axe for each person.
- Learn to recognize dangerous snow slopes.
- Carry a climbing rope and know the correct use of rope and ice axe.

- ***In case of rescue service being required, dial 999 and ask for the police. Follow the instructions you receive.***

Just in case you *do* get into trouble, the recognised **mountain distress signals** are six long whistle blasts or torch flashes, repeated at one minute intervals. Alternatively, you can shout. Continue to repeat the distress signals until your rescuers are with you. The recognised answer is three return signals.

Waymarking, maps and grading

Very few footpaths in the Scottish Highlands are **waymarked** in any way at all. Where waymarking does exist, then I have highlighted the existence of such signs at the appropriate point in the main walk descriptions.

Ordnance Survey (OS) **maps** are among the best of their kind in the world. They are essential for walking in the Scottish Highlands, the 1:50,000 Landranger series being ideal. The maps reproduced in this book should be adequate in most situations but, on the high mountains, where navigation could be a problem in adverse weather, it is advisable to carry the full map sheet. At the beginning of each walk I have specified the relevant sheet number.

I have also allocated a **grade** to each walk, dependent on distance covered, height gained, steepness, technical difficulty and the roughness of the terrain. Six basic terms have been used: easy; easy-moderate; moderate; moderate-strenuous; strenuous; very strenuous. This is followed by a brief overview of what to expect. Most of the hill (mountain) walks have been graded strenuous or very strenuous but even these, as mentioned previously, are well within the capabilities of experienced walkers.

Where to stay

The main village or town from where the relevant car tour begins is often the place to base yourself for the walks. I also have mentioned the nearest accommodation for each walk at the top of the page, in the 'How to get there' section.

The other consideration regarding where to say is the type of accommodation you require. There are three main types of accommodation to choose from in the Highlands: hotel, youth hostel and bed and breakfast (B&B). They all vary in quality and price. B&B in private homes is the most widely available type of accommodation, where you can expect to pay £15-£25 per person per night. In the more remote areas there maybe no choice.

Organisation of the walks

There are 30 main walks in this book, spread across the entire Highlands of Scotland, from The Trossachs in the south to Sutherland in the north. Each walk is accessible from a parking place on one of the ten car tours. Moreover, almost all of the starting places for the walks can be reached by public transport of some kind, frequently the daily Postbus (except Sundays).

I have devised an average of three walks for each car tour, although the more popular and easily-accessible areas, such as The Trossachs and Glen Coe, have four, while the remoter areas may have only two.

*Walk 5:
approaching
The Cobbler*

Begin by taking a look at the fold-out map and noting the walks that are nearest to you. Then turn to the appropriate route description where, at the top of the page, you will find planning information: distance, time, grade, equipment, how to get there, and suggestions for shorter and longer walks. Many alternatives are possible: these might be simple extensions or shortenings of the main walk, while other recommendations could be different walks altogether, but located nearby. This gives a degree of flexibility and allows you to tailor each walk as prevailing weather conditions, or your abilities, may dictate. *(But note that most of the nearby routes I suggest will not be shown in full on the map extract for the walks in this book; you will need to buy the full OS sheet.)*

Throughout each walk description, **cumulative times** are given for reaching certain landmarks. These are only estimates, based on my own performance, and *making no allowance for rest stops.* It would be a good idea to compare your pace with mine on a fairly short walk before tackling a longer hike.

Below is a **key to the symbols** used on the maps; most of them also appear on the far right of every OS sheet.

A826 — main roads (dashed lines where narrow)	—50— contours (in 10 m intervals)	▲ youth hostel
B885 secondary roads	△ •427 cairn.spot height	✕ picnic site
narrow road, over 4 m (12 ft) wide.unfenced	rock outcrop	golf course
narrow road, lane	cliffs	✆ public telephone
- - - - footpath	scree	+ site of monument
main walk, with start-ing point and direction	railway stations: local.principal	+ church:
- - -→ alternative route	tourist information: all year.seasonal	with tower. with spire
boundaries:	viewpoint	MS milestone
national.district	P parking	PC public toilets
national or forest park	camp/caravan site	PH pub
Forestry Commission or National Trust		P post office
		CH clubhouse
		page reference

Access

There is, in effect, no law of trespass in Scotland. Scots have long enjoyed a 'freedom to roam' that is the envy of walkers south of the border. However, you must respect the few restrictions to access that *do* exist and which are normally imposed only at certain times of the year, and on a few private estates. This will help prevent conflict and maintain a cordial relationship between walkers and landowners.

Specifically, the activities which can affect access for walkers are deerstalking, normally mid-August to mid October, grouse shooting, between 12th August and 10 December, and lambing in the springtime. Such activities are usually well advertised at the perimeters of the estates affected.

Munros

'Munro-collecting' has reached obsessive proportions among hillwalkers in Scotland. A Munro is simply defined as a separate mountain over 3000ft (914m). Sir Hugh Munro first listed 283 in 1891 but, over the years, the list has been subject to tampering. Today the Scottish Mountaineering Club recognises 284 such summits. A total of eight Munros are included in the main walk described in this book, with suggestions to include more if you have the energy.

Nuisances

There is just one and it's tiny! *Culicoides impunctatus* is just 2mm long but the Highland midge can be present in persistent, man-eating swarms. She (for it is the female that bites) has been the ruin of many a Highland summer holiday but, based on the precept that the most effective defence comes from knowing your enemy, have listed a few useful facts.

— The midge season runs from late May to early September, reaching misery-inducing levels during July and August.

— Midges are most active on still, overcast days and least active in wind or in bright sunshine.

— They are more likely to be encountered at lower levels and under trees.

— They are attracted to dark colours.

There are several effective chemical repellents and sprays available. I have found 'Jungle Formula' to be one of the best.

1 PEDESTRIAN PATH AND CYCLEWAY TO STRATHYRE

See also photograph page 18 (top)

Distance: 13.5km/8.5mi; 3h45min

Grade: a moderate, but easy to follow walk along the course of an old railway

Equipment: no special equipment necessary. OS Landranger sheet 57

How to get there and return: 🚗 Park in Callander (Car tour 1), or 🚌 to Callander. See timetables at the Tourist Office for bus or Postbus return from Strathyre. Nearest accommodation in Callander.

Shorter walks: Follow the main walk to Loch Lubnaig and return the same way (up to 3h). Or walk up to Bracklinn Falls, by taking the lane to the north of Callander, then the path from the car park to the falls (1h45min return).

Longer walks: Follow the main walk as described, but continue to Balquidder and Rob Roy's Grave using OS Landranger sheet 51 (17.5km/11mi; 4h45min). Or combine with Walk 2 (21.5km/13.5mi; 7h40min, but note grade and equipment specifications on page 55).

Plans are currently underway to establish a cycle and pedestrian way into the mountains from the north of Glasgow. Otherwise known as the 'Railway Path Project', much of this route will follow the track beds of the old railways of the Southern Highlands.

Whilst disused railways can today provide excellent tracks and paths for cyclists and walkers, it is perhaps little consolation for what was sacrificed. Up until the 1960s, Scotland and the rest of Britain had an extensive railway network but, with the Beeching Act, transport policy shifted overwhelmingly in favour of the motor car. For much of rural Britain train travel is now a thing of the past.

The walk described below follows the section of way-marked path from Callander through a beautiful forested glen to the village of Strathyre. This countryside was once

Ben Ledi from Glen Finglas (below the mountain's west face)

a familiar pleasure for the passengers on the Caledonian Railway trains, steaming their way to Oban.

Start out by walking west along the A84 from Callander. The path begins on your left, just past the Coppice Hotel, at a signpost for 'BALQUIDDER 10, STRATHYRE 8' (miles). You may find it worthwhile pausing at the old signals here which, like the steam locomotives which some of us still remember, provide a brief opportunity to indulge in a bit of romance and nostalgia. Along the way, railway enthusiasts will no doubt find further excuses to linger; there are bridges, arches, displaced sleepers and old buffers to investigate. For the first mile, the trackbed is raised up, originally with the purpose of carrying the railway over the water meadows of the **River Teith**. This makes for very pleasurable walking, where picturesque Ben Ledi rises up ahead of you (photograph page 18, top). The trail is easy to follow, with no route-finding problems, and this is true of the Railway Path almost all the way to Strathyre. The chances are you will meet more cyclists than walkers.

Having reached the A821 (**25min**), you will encounter some site-specific sculpture, recently commissioned, including a wall which reflects not only a railway heritage but also the undulating flow of the nearby river.

Cross the road and enter a more wooded section, above the left bank of the Garbh Uisge. In springtime, the embankments are splashed with the colours of pretty woodland flowers including wood anemone, primrose and bluebells. There is a place on the right for a proper view of the river above the **Falls of Leny** (**50min**) where, in autumn, you might just spot a salmon leaping. Bear left following the trail through the oak trees, departing briefly from the course of the railway but continuing along the official cycleway.

A little further on you pass to the left of a BRIDGE (**1h 05min**). The path up to Ben Ledi (Walk 2) starts opposite the bridge. From here follow the surfaced track ahead. A signpost, 'STRATHYRE 4, CALLANDER 4' (**1h10min**) — suggests that you are halfway through the walk, but you are *not!* Where the river meets **Loch Lubnaig**, there is a feeling of

being less confined, and the tarmac surface gives way to a hard-pack track. The course of the old railway continues by the west shore of the loch, through the forested glen

As you draw opposite a large house situated on the east shore, at **Ardchullarie More** (**2h25min**), take the path that twists left uphill, joining a forestry track. Looking out across the loch, close to where the track reaches its highest point, you have a chance to savour views of true sylvan charm.

At a flat grassy area where sheep graze by the loch shore, follow the track down to rejoin the course of the old railway (now a farm track) by a bridge over the **Allt Mòr** burn. Go through a wooden gate below the farmhouse at **Laggan** (**3h**), after which the route continues up a hillside again, to join another forestry track (**3h15min**).

Beyond Strathyre CARAVAN PARK, at the north end of Loch Lubnaig, the walk nears its end on a pleasant country lane. Approaching the village, an obvious path on the right leads over a suspension footbridge, before emerging at the main road in **Strathyre**, opposite the Munro Hotel (**3h45min**).

Before catching the bus back, I can recommend the experience of a traditional country cottage cream tea at the An Carraig Tea Room. The ritual comes complete with bone china tea cups and home-baked goodies, a very British end to a very perfect day.

2 BEN LEDI

See map pages 52-53; see also photographs pages 18 (top) and 51

Distance: 9.5km/6mi; 4h20min

Grade: a steep and moderately-strenuous climb of 755m/2476ft, but otherwise straightforward, following a well-used path. Competence with a compass is advisable (see notes on 'Walking').

Equipment: 3- or 4-season walking boots and wind/waterproofs. OS Landranger sheet 57

How to get there and return: 🚘 Park in the lay-by by 'Stank Road' (Car tour 1); or 🚌 to/from Callander, then Postbus or on foot (see Walk 1) to 'Stank Road' (4km WNW). Nearest accommodation in Callander.

Shorter walks: Climb as high as you wish towards the summit and return the same way; perhaps combine this with the first 1h05min of Walk 1.

Longer walk: Link Walks 1 and 2 together (21.5km/13.5mi; 7h40min).

Ben Ledi is the mountain by which Callander identifies itself as 'The Gateway to the Highlands'. Certainly coming from the south or east of Scotland, the ben is very much the beginning of the mountains. The climb to its summit is a wonderful 'first' for those unfamiliar with the Highlands, with strikingly contrasting views as a reward.

Begin from the BRIDGE over the Garbh Uisge, on the 'Stank Road', just north of the Falls of Leny. The FC have waymarked the route through Strathyre Forest using a 'boot' symbol. They have also laid timbers over the soggier sections, so your feet should stay dry, at least at first!

The path crosses a forestry access track before reaching a BURN (**35min**) at a gap in the trees higher up. Turn left and follow the path upstream, onto the open mountainside. The views are much better here, no longer obscured by the year-round blanket of conifers. The going can be quite wet underfoot on this section. Continue down a bank, to cross the upper

The summit of Ben Ledi. As you might expect of such a vantage point, where the highlands meet the lowlands, the panorama of barren mountain summits to the north contrasts in a particularly striking way with the flat fertile plains of the south. On a clear day, Stirling Castle and the Wallace Monument are visible and occasionally even Arthur's Seat in Edinburgh can be seen. Looking north, many of the most distinctive mountains in the Southern Highlands extend across the skyline. It can be fun trying to identify them all, and even more fun to try and pronounce their names! The Arrochar Alps, including Ben Narnain and The Cobbler (Walk 5) rise to the northwest, while to the north (the view in this photograph) are Stob Binnein, Ben More, Ben Vorlich and Stùc a' Chroin.

55

reaches of the burn (**50min**). On the far side, go over a STILE, bearing left towards the southeast ridge of Ben Ledi.

Where the gradient eases, and just beyond a LARGE CAIRN, you will find a SMALLER CAIRN at about the 590m contour. Here, turn right and follow the clearly-defined ridge rising to the northwest. The well-worn path follows a line of rusty FENCE POSTS up along the crest of the ridge.

After one or two false summits, keep climbing until you reach an obvious IRON CROSS on a schistose outcrop near the top. This memorial, to Sergeant Harry Lowrie, who died on duty with the Killin mountain rescue team, is a humble reminder that there are those prepared to risk their own lives to save yours. We hillwalkers owe it to these selfless souls to ensure we are properly prepared and equipped for the Scottish mountains.

The trig pillar on the SUMMIT OF **Ben Ledi** (**2h05min**) lies at 879m, failing by just 35m to reach Munro status. Apart from the wonderful views shown on pages 54-55, there is wildlife to be seen here, too; I have been entertained by joyful mountain hares in spring, as well as ptarmigans in pure white plumage in winter — as immovable as the unmelted snow that they pretend to imitate. In the years to come, birch, rowan and hazel will begin to spread across the lower west-facing slopes of Ben Ledi and around Glen Finglas (photograph page 51). The estate, recently acquired by The Woodland Trust, is now being managed for the regeneration of deciduous trees, which should in turn encourage a more diverse flora and fauna.

To descend the mountain, continue north and then northwest, again following the line of rusty FENCE POSTS. Where the path forks, go right, away from the posts, on a grassy little-worn path that leads to the COL (**2h45min**) at the top of Stank Glen. From here go east and downstream beside a burn, to reach a STILE over sheep fencing, just above the top of the plantation trees (**3h05min**).

In the forest again, a waymarked path follows the **Stank Burn** through the conifers and felled areas to a forest track (**3h30min**). Follow it to the right for just a few metres, then continue down a rough track to the left. At a more established forest track (**3h40min**), turn right, cross the burn, then follow a waymarked path on the left. It is worth pausing briefly as you descend, to view the lovely waterfalls on the left. On nearing the house at **Stank** (**3h55min**), follow a track down to the cycle and pedestrian way, again beside the **Garbh Uisge**. Continue south, recrossing the river at the BRIDGE by the parking place (**4h20min**).

3 BEN A'AN

Distance: 3km/2mi; 1h45min

Grade: a very short walk involving an easy, if quite abrupt climb of 350m/1148ft on a well-worn path.

Equipment: except during dry summer weather, 3-season walking boots are recommended. OS Landranger sheet 57

How to get there and return: 🚗 Park at the FC car park for Ben A'an, by the northwest corner of Loch Achray (Car tour 1). 🚐 The Postbus between Callander and Aberfoyle or 'The Trossachs Trundler' will drop you off/collect you there. Nearest accommodation at Loch Achray Hotel.

Longer walk: Climb rugged Ben Venue, on the south side of Loch Katrine, waymarked through Achray Forest from the Loch Achray Hotel (10.5km/6.5mi; 4h return).

What is generally referred to as The Trossachs ('the Bristly Country') falls roughly within a triangle between Callander, Aberfoyle and Loch Katrine. The Forestry Commission have their own name for this rugged and picturesque area: the Queen Elizabeth Forest Park, which also encompasses a much wider area to the south and west. However, The Trossachs proper is really just the small area of lochside forest and crags below Ben A'an and above the east shore of Loch Katrine.

If you have time for just one short walk in Rob Roy country, then make it this one. Watching the sun go down across the lovely waters of Loch Katrine is a special treat, so the short climb up to Ben A'an is just perfect for an invigorating evening walk. In summertime, there will be plenty of light after sunset for a brisk descent to be made perfectly safely.

Begin the ascent from the FC car park, following the sign 'FOOTPATH TO BEN A'AN' on the opposite side of the road. After just a few minutes the path begins to follow the left bank of a burn. Among a tangle of roots, rocks and deciduous trees, there is a FOOTBRIDGE (**10min**) to be crossed from where, above the opposite bank, your endeavour becomes a little more energetic.

It is worth a slight detour out to the VIEWPOINT on the left (**15min**) to view the bold, craggy summit of Ben A'an, seen rising in due prominence above the tops of the trees! Try not to be put off by the seemingly invincible task ahead of you; this sharp cone of schistose rock is not really as daunting as it looks.

57

On Ben A'an: having just emerged from the plantation, walkers head towards the summit cone.

Walk on up through the larch trees, stepping across one or two intervening burns on the way, before eventually emerging from the trees in a BRACKEN-COVERED CLEARING (**30min**). You are now much closer to your objective, although from here the going gets a bit tougher. The steep eroded footpath up the east side of the crags begins easily enough as a series of rocky steps through birch scrub, but then becomes a little more awkward as it crosses boulders higher up.

The wild moorland up here can be an exquisite purple-pink sea of heather, fulfilling many foreign visitors' expectation of the Scottish countryside. To avoid disappointment however, remember that such a vivid and colourful display is only possible in late summer, when the bell heather and ling are in flower.

On reaching a pale QUARTZITE BOULDER, which resembles a giant snowball, the path forks (**45min**). Take the right-hand option for the least steep final push up to the summit. Further on the path twists back sharply left just before you reach the top. The SUMMIT OF **Ben A'an** (**55min**) is the most magnificent vantage point, and the view a reward quite out of proportion to the little effort invested. No wonder then that Ben A'an is just about the most popular hillwalk in the area. This lofty perch above Loch Katrine provides the very best opportunity to contemplate the true heart of The Trossachs. Below flourishes a predominantly deciduous forest, hugging the shore of the loch and the rugged mountain slopes that lie between here and Ben Venue, the mountain looming higher still, just 3km to the southwest. Further west, beyond the much-visited and celebrated waters of Loch Katrine, the Arrochar Alps display their distinguished peaks on the Argyll skyline. It is tempting to linger a long while and take it all in, but it would be wise not to begin your descent too long after sunset.

Retrace your steps to the A821 at **Loch Achray** (**1h 45min**), carefully negotiating the rocky section just below the summit. Stumbles are more likely to occur, and loose rocks are more easily dislodged, on the way down.

4 WILDLIFE RAMBLE ON THE 'BONNIE BANKS'

See also photograph page 18 (bottom)

Distance: 9km/5.6mi; 3h

Grade: an easy walk on good clear paths, including an RSPB nature trail

Equipment: no special equipment necessary. OS Landranger sheet 56

How to get there and return: 🚗 Park at the large public car park by the Inversnaid Hotel, at the end of the minor road which joins the B829 from Aberfoyle (Car tour 1). 🚐 daily Postbus from/back to Aberfoyle. Nearest accommodation at Inversnaid Hotel and Inversnaid Lodge.

Longer walks: From Inversnaid, head north or south following the West Highland Way as far as you like, before returning to Inversnaid along the shore of Loch Lomond. Another rewarding possibility involves a pathless ascent of Cruachan, beginning from the car park at Arklet Bridge, then descending to the loch shore via the Gleann Gaoithe track and returning by the West Highland Way (8km/5mi; 3h30min).

'What would the world be once bereft
of wet and wilderness?
O let them be left, wilderness and wet;
Long live the weeds and the wilderness yet.'

Gerard Manley Hopkins' poem 'Inversnaid' can be interpreted as a Victorian plea for conservation. It was very much inspired by his wanderings along the Snaid Burn. Indeed, there can be few better ways to spend a leisurely morning or afternoon; difficult to believe that, as the buzzard flies, you are less than 30 miles north of Glasgow!

The route I have suggested is an easy walk, although you can pretty much please yourself just where you choose to wander around the lovely hamlet of Inversnaid. There is much of interest here, plenty to satisfy budding ornithologists and nature lovers, as well as those following in the footsteps of Rob Roy and others who are looking for subjects for the camera.

Start walking north from the hotel car park, following the WEST HIGHLAND WAY along the shore of Loch Lomond. The 'Way' was Scotland's first officially-designated long distance footpath. Every year, thousands undertake the challenge on the 154km/95mi trek, beginning just north of Glasgow and finishing in the shadow of Ben Nevis (Walk 11), usually about a week later. Almost as many again manage only part of it, underestimating the task and the blistering punishment to soft feet.

There is an information panel by the hotel highlighting the bird life in the RSPB reserve. These semi-naturalised woods provide the ideal habitat for resident species such as blue tit, great tit and robin which in spring are joined by migrants such as pied flycatcher, redstart, willow warbler and wood warbler. It is well worthwhile carrying a pair of binoculars. The reserve is also rich in plant life. In spring, bluebells, primroses, wood sorrels and wood anemones are widespread.

Just beyond the BOATHOUSE (**10min**), turn right off the WHW, following the signposted nature trail. This well-engineered path heads up into the birchwood and then, higher up, more dense oak woodland. Look out for the remains of a small settlement here, called **Cladachbeag**. Still visible are three ruined buildings, now being reclaimed by mosses and ferns.

After crossing a small burn, you climb up to the highest point on the trail and the main VIEWPOINT (**25min**). This gives superb views of Loch Lomond, as well as the surrounding mountains including Ben Lomond. Golden eagles are occasionally seen from here. Only part of Loch Lomond is in view — not surprising, since it is 40km/25mi long and the largest area of freshwater in Britain.

Continue the walk along the trail, descending at a footbridge over a burn and past the remains of another old building. As you may have guessed, Scotland's mountain areas were, up to the 19th century, far more densely populated than they are today (see Preface). Continue to descend and rejoin the WHW by the loch shore. Here turn right and walk about 300m north to ROB ROY'S CAVE (**50min**). From above, the entrance can be difficult to locate, although someone has painted 'CAVE' on a rock. Rob Roy, Scotland's Highland Robin Hood, is said to have once sheltered here, having successfully eluded capture by the Hanoverian troops. Apparently he was led to the cave by Inversnaid's famous wild goats. Today, these creatures continue to forage in the undergrowth on the reserve and are frequently encountered by visitors to Inversnaid.

Return to the HOTEL CAR PARK (**1h15min**) and, from the south side of the building, you should join everyone else in admiring the impressive waterfall. Then climb the path on the left-hand side of the falls and head upriver through the trees, to join the road. Continue along the road, now high up on the bank of the **Snaid Burn**, passing Inversnaid Lodge. The lodge can be recommended, not only for its excellent photography workshops, but also for the high quality of B&B accommodation.

Just beyond ARKLET BRIDGE, you will come to a very picturesque church, now a Boys' Brigade activity centre. A little further on, the road crosses the Snaid Burn, a good spot to see dippers and grey wagtails. The remains of the old garrison are here too, near the primary school, now integrated into the buildings of GARRISON FARM (**1h50min**). The Hanoverian troops were stationed here in the 18th century to subdue the marauding MacGregors, but to little effect!

If you are lucky enough to enjoy the benefit of morning sunshine and a light wind, it is rewarding to walk a further 1.5km east along the road, to just beyond the dam at **Loch Arklet** (**2h15min**). The Arrochar Alps provide the perfect backdrop for a photograph across the water (see bottom of page 18). Together with Loch Katrine, Loch Arklet serves as a reservoir for Glasgow's water supply.

The open hill slopes of Glen Arklet are also good places to watch and listen for birds. Among those regularly seen and heard from the road are the black grouse, as well as the curlew, woodcock, buzzard, short-eared owl and hen harrier. Return to the HOTEL CAR PARK (**3h**).

Loch Lomond from above the RSPB reserve at Inversnaid

5 THE COBBLER

See photograph page 49

Distance: 9km/5.5mi; 4h40min (5h10min, including the central peak)

Grade: a very strenuous walk, involving a total ascent of 900m/2950ft, with optional scrambling on the summit. Competence with a compass is advisable (see notes on 'Walking').

Equipment: 3- or 4-season walking boots and wind/waterproofs. OS Landranger sheet 56

How to get there and return: 🚗 Park in the car park at Succoth, beside Loch Long (Car tour 2). 🚌 Coaches from Glasgow and Crianlarich to/from Arrochar (1km southeast). 🚂 Train from Glasgow to/from Tarbet (2.5km east), or train to Tarbet from stations further north on the Fort William line. Nearest accommodation at Arrochar; YH at Ardgarten

Shorter walk: Having reached the small dam across the Allt a' Bhalachain (1h), turn southeast and head back down through the plantation to a forest track just above Loch Long, thus returning to Succoth (4.5km/3mi; 2h20min). A moderate but steep climb of 390m/1280ft, followed by the same descent, completes this short circuit.

Ben Arthur, or The Cobbler as it is more commonly known, is one of the most striking mountains in the Southern Highlands. It is very popular with Glasgow hillwalkers and climbers yet, failing by 30m/100ft to reach qualifying height, Munroists often ignore it in favour of other less exciting mountains of the Arrochar Alps.

It is the unusual profile of the schist outcrops on its summit ridge that have given the mountain its name. The rock strata, folded by geological forces and sculptured by millions of years of erosion, are said to resemble a cobbler bent over his last.

Begin the walk from the car park by the shore of **Loch Long**. Cross the road and take the track by the 'ARGYLL FOREST PARK' sign, passing in front of a mountain rescue donation cairn (loose change always gratefully accepted). Right from the start you will be trudging steeply upward, following a line of CONCRETE BLOCKS which once carried an old hydroelectric railway. Within a few minutes you cross a forestry track. Continuing the climb, height is gained quickly on the open hill up to a point where an obvious JUNCTION OF PATHS is reached (**45min**). The path to Beinn Narnain, a Munro, continues upwards. However, instead follow the better path across the flank of the hillside to the left. From here, it will be obvious just how Loch Long got its name.

Looking upstream from a small dam breaching the **Allt a' Bhalachain** (**1h**; 'Weir' on the OS map), Ben Arthur completely dominates the skyline and, for all mountain lovers, will prove an irresistible lure. With a stretch of the imagination, perhaps you can just see a cobbler!

Follow a path up the right-hand side of the stream to reach the two huge Narnain boulders (**1h20min**), almost as notable a feature of the area as the *beinn* of the same name and to whose cliffs they once belonged, until torn away perhaps by the icy claws of some ancient glacier. Rock climbers can often be seen practising here.

Following the path upstream, leave the Narnain pair and rock-hop across the Allt a' Bhalachain. After traversing wet moorland on the other side, a more clearly-defined path up ever-steeper outcrops becomes evident. The effects of decades of trampling boots have taken their inevitable erosive toll on the ascent path and have done nothing to ease the gruelling push up towards the summit. Beware of loose, easily dislodged rocks.

On gaining the SUMMIT RIDGE (**2h20min**), turn right to climb the easiest of the three distinct peaks, the north peak. At the TOP (**The Cobbler's Last; 2h30min**), stay well away from the edge, especially if you suffer from vertigo! The view from here is magnificent. The highest of the Arrochar Alps, Beinn Ime, lies immediately north and rugged Beinn Narnain rises to the east. The conspicuous mountain cone seen on the skyline above the east shore of Loch Lomond is Ben Lomond, Scotland's most southerly Munro.

The descent follows the same route. But if you are feeling adventurous and enjoy scrambling, first walk south-west, via the point where you first gained the ridge. Then go up along the ridge path to the central and highest peak. Gaining this precarious summit involves an unparalleled test of nerve — an ordeal that was once the preserve of Campbell chiefs, dedicated to proving their manhood! From the base of the pinnacle, climb up through a rock window (**Argyll's Eyeglass**) and, from an exposed narrow ledge, scramble up to the TOP of **The Cobbler** (**2h45min**). Return *very carefully*. Then walk back to the COL below the north peak and retrace steps down Ben Arthur, to return to car park at **Loch Long** (**4h40min**).

6 RANNOCH MOOR AND THE BLACK MOUNT

See also photograph pages 68-69

Distance: 14.5km/9mi; 4h

Grade: a moderate walk along an easy to follow 'drove road' with little gradient

Equipment: no special equipment necessary, but walking boots, food and extra clothing are recommended. OS Landranger sheet 50

How to get there and return: 🚗 Park at the car park near Victoria Bridge (Car tour 2). 🚌 Bus or 🚂 train to/from Bridge of Orchy on the Glasgow/Edinburgh to Fort William lines, then 🚐 Postbus or on foot to/from Victoria Bridge (6km). Nearest accommodation at Inveroran Hotel and Bridge of Orchy Hotel/Bunkhouse.

Longer walk: It is particularly satisfying to continue north on the drove road from Bà Bridge, walking on to the Kings House Hotel, Glen Coe (15.5km/9.5mi; 4h20min), assuming you can organise transport back.

There are very few possibilities for walkers to explore the labyrinth of peat banks, streams, *lochans* and bogs which characterise Rannoch Moor. First impressions suggest a flat terrain ideal for walking, but progress on foot is typically slow, uncomfortable and ridden with obstacles. However, there is at the edge of Rannoch Moor an old drove road (cattle-moving road) which offers walkers a trouble-free route across the moor, to experience its desolate beauty without problems.

Begin the walk from the CAR PARK near the end of the A8005 road. Continue along the road, crossing VICTORIA BRIDGE (**5min**), from where there is a lovely view upstream beyond the pine trees, to the mountains of Glen Kinglass. Go over a stile at FOREST LODGE to gain the signposted 'Drove Road to Glen Coe'. This is now part of the West Highland Way, the long-distance footpath from Glasgow to Fort William, a marathon trek growing in popularity.

Heading north, ignore a track on the right leading to

Rannoch Moor

Rannoch Moor and Stob à Choire Odhair, the Munro climbed in Walk 7

Black Mount House (**25min**). You can establish a good pace on this dry, level track, which is cobbled in places. The gradient rises gently, alongside spruce enclosures, and skirts below the **Black Mount**, the range of mountains which rim the western edge of Rannoch Moor. Beinn Toaig presents a rugged façade on the left, masking Stob à Choire Odhair (Walk 7) from view. To your right, the moor extends far to the east, a vast flat tableland that is in fact 300m/1000ft above sea level.

Traversing the open moorland, the track bridges a number of attractive little burns. It is fun to lean over and drop your sandwich crumbs into the water, waiting for the next brown trout to dart out from under the arch of a bridge. Such simple pleasures often become necessary distractions, so wherever you are in the Scottish Highlands, always allow extra time for the enjoyment of nature.

There is a PLANTATION on the left (**1h20min**) and soon after, another on the right; both seem somewhat incongruous, isolated as they are amid the desolation. One thing to be said in favour of these islands of monocultured spruce is the shelter they provide for small birds, whose springtime song brings melody to an otherwise silent moor. Just beyond the trees, the track comes next to **Lochan Mhic Pheadair Ruaidhe** (**1h40min**), a pleasant spot to pause and watch herons stalking its shallow waters for small trout. There are ducks to be seen here too.

BÀ BRIDGE (**2h**) is the turning-back point of this walk, and the River Bà provides the loveliest foreground to all the peaks of the Black Mount which encircle the broad corrie on the left. It is a memorable situation, so wild that even the engineered drove road and the formality of a

nearby plantation cannot diminish one's sense of solitude. Plan to linger here a good while before returning the same way to VICTORIA BRIDGE (**4h**). *Do not* be fooled into thinking you can return on the trail marked 'Old Military Road' on the OS map; it does not exist in any viable form!

7 STOB À CHOIRE ODHAIR

See map opposite; see also photographs pages 64 and 65

Distance: 13km/8mi; 5h15min

Grade: a strenuous and steep ascent of 760m/2494ft, but with no technical difficulty; wet in places on descent. Competence with a compass is advisable (see notes on 'Walking').

Equipment: 3- or 4-season walking boots and wind/waterproofs. OS Landranger sheet 50

How to get there and return: 🚗 Park at the car park near Victoria Bridge (Car tour 2). 🚌 Bus or 🚂 train to/from Bridge of Orchy on the Glasgow/Edinburgh to Fort William lines, then 🚐 Postbus or on foot to/from Victoria Bridge (6km). Nearest accommodation at Inveroran Hotel and Bridge of Orchy Hotel/Bunkhouse.

Shorter walks: Return by ascent route on or before reaching the summit. You can avoid the mountain altogether by walking up into the Coire Toaig only, returning the same way. Walk 6 is also an easier alternative.

The view of the Black Mount, from where the A82 road dissects the *lochan*-pitted tableland of Rannoch Moor, is one of the most celebrated in Scotland, having appeared on everything from calendars to packets of shortbread. This mountain walk explores one of the southernmost peaks of the Black Mount range and is memorable for its outstanding summit views. From Stob à Choire Odhair, the true extent of Rannoch Moor is seen to tremendous effect. Such a worthy objective deserves a fine, clear day, so stay tuned to weather forecasts.

At 945m/3100ft, Stob à Choire Odhair is a Munro (Scottish mountain over 3,000ft) and as such demands appropriate respect — see 'Walking' notes. Yet despite its lofty status, this mountain is in fact among the easiest Munros to 'bag', making an ideal first if you have not climbed any before.

Begin the walk at the CAR PARK on the A8005, just before the road terminates. Continue along the road to cross VICTORIA BRIDGE (**5min**). From here, the scene up-river into Glen Kinglass has much of the essence of the Southern and Central Highlands.

A little further on, turn left in front of FOREST LODGE, leaving the road for a good track beneath Scots pines. Follow signposting 'FOOTPATH TO LOCH ETIVE BY GLEN KINGLASS'. This track follows the course of the river, the **Abhainn Shira**, upstream.

At the Glasgow University Mountaineering Club HUT (**35min**), leave the track for a path on the right. After following the east bank of a stream, the Allt Toaig, to the bottom of a prominent WATERFALL (**1h**), keep to the increasingly rougher path up into the **Coire Toaig**.

About 800m/half a mile beyond the falls, ford a small

BURN (**1h15min**). At this point, you should leave the path that continues into the higher reaches of the corrie and instead pursue a less-defined route up through the heather on your right. This path rises sharply on the steep south shoulder of the mountainside where, higher up, a well-engineered stalkers' path becomes more apparent. From here on the climb — an endless series of zigzags — will render you breathless at times. There are no obstacles or technical problems involved, so height is gained quickly, and with each step the views are more impressive. On your left, a close neighbour, Stob Ghabhar, assumes a particularly commanding presence. If you are here in springtime, it will be evident that the shadowy recesses of its deeply-scalloped east-facing corrie can hold snow well into summer.

When the steepness of the climb at last relents (**2h 20min**), it is necessary to continue across a boulder field. Although the path here is less obvious, your route to the summit remains straightforward. Look out for that high-rise chameleon of the bird world, the ptarmigan, the sight of which is a good indication that you are above 750m/ 2500ft. It is fun to try and get close to these birds, but the fact that they seem so reluctant to fly off in panic is more a demonstration of their reliance on camouflage (their plumage changes with the degree of snow cover) than of a fearless disposition.

The SUMMIT CAIRN on **Stob à Choire Odhair** (**2h45min**) is located above the rocky north face of the mountain, from where, suddenly upon arrival, Rannoch Moor is revealed — the vast flat bogland shown on pages 64 and 65. Stretching northeastwards for many miles and perforated with numerous *lochans,* on a sunny day it displays a desolate kind of beauty which, from a distance, effectively disguises an unnavigable labyrinth of peat hags, stagnant pools and stumble-inducing heathery tussocks. With the exception of a few established paths and tracks (des-

The mountains of Glen Kinglass, from Victoria Bridge (starting point for Walks 6 and 7)

cribed in Walk 6), it is a wilderness out of bounds for the walker.

The summit is also an exceptional vantage point for viewing the surrounding mountains. You can see Stob Ghabhar at its best from here, while the lovely alpine-like profile which dominates the northern horizon is Bidean nam Bian, Argyll's highest mountain.

Leave the summit by following a rough path along the ridge that runs west, directly toward Stob Ghabhar. The descent traverses a few rocky outcrops, but the ridge is broad, route-finding unproblematic, and the setting magnificent — in my view infinitely preferable to the more direct, but knee-punishing way down on the south side (the ascent route in reverse). Do be wary, however, of stumbling on easily-dislodged stones.

Shortly before arriving at a col, there is an awkward rock-step to negotiate; the less agile can easily bypass this to the right. After passing the cairn on the COL (660m; **3h30min**), turn left to cross wet grass at the top of the **Coire Toaig**. Continue walking down through the corrie, soon gaining a more obvious path that stays close to the uppermost reaches of the Allt Toaig.

After another 2km/1.25mi you will have completed a most enjoyable circuit, having returned to the burn where previously you left the corrie path for the ascent (**4h 20min**). From here, simply retrace your footsteps back to VICTORIA BRIDGE and the CAR PARK (**5h15min**).

8 FOLLOWING THE PASSAGE OF STEAM THROUGH GLEN DOCHART AND GLEN OGLE

Distance: 24.5km/15.2mi; 6h10min

Grade: a moderate but long walk, first following a peaceful country lane and later the course of old railways and forestry tracks

Equipment: no special equipment necessary, but 3-season walking boots recommended. Unreliable availability of refreshments along the way, so pack your own food. OS Landranger sheet 51

How to get there and return: 🚗 Park in Killin near the Falls of Dochart (Car tour 3). 🚌 Regular coach connections with Stirling, Edinburgh, Glasgow and Fort William. Postbuses from Crianlarich and Callander. Nearest accommodation in Killin.

Shorter walks: From old Killin Junction station, return to Killin by continuing along the trackbed of the railway (17km/10.6mi; 4h25min). For a shorter walk still, simply walk along the old Killin branch railway from Killin, turning back again from the old station (10km/6.2mi; 2h20min).

Before setting off, you should allow time to linger a while at the Falls of Dochart (see Car tour 3). Then, turning away from the inevitable crowds of sightseers, this walk explores the southernmost sections of Glen Dochart and Glen Ogle. Both once carried the railways of the Callander and Oban line, with the Killin branch joining the main line from the south at old Killin Junction station. Their trackbeds now provide ideal routes for walkers. For the future, it is hoped this section of old railway can be joined with the trackbed south of Strathyre (Walk 1), as well as with a route to be opened up further to the north, thus creating a new long-distance path for cyclists and walkers, to be called the Central Highland Way.

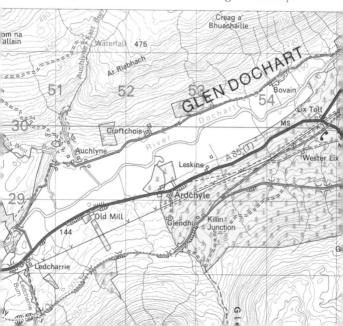

As far as Ledcharrie, this walk follows the recommended detour for Car tour 3 in Glen Dochart. **Start the walk** just north of the TOURIST INFORMATION CENTRE. Head southwest and follow Craignavie Road, on the north side of the river. You pass Manse Road on your right (**10min**) and soon leave the houses of Killin behind. At a GATE (**20min**) the lane comes close to the beautiful river on your left. Pass through a second GATE (**40min**) and, beyond the trees, the glen broadens, to give fine views across the river valley. Looking southwest, you cannot fail to notice a most distinctive landmark, a fine twinning of mountain peaks, Ben More and Stob Binnien. South of where you stand, no mountain in Britain is higher than Ben More.

In **Glen Dochart**, look out for herons and dippers by the river, deer on the mountainside on the right and buzzards circling the skies above BOVAIN FARM (**55min**). At **Auchlyne** (**1h50min**), cross both the East and West burns and follow the road to the left, beneath canopies of oak and birch. The parapet of the bridge over the main **River Dochart** (**2h10min**) is a glorious spot to enjoy the river and its wildlife. Sometimes there are anglers here

Ben More and Stob Binnein from the lane in Glen Dochart (above) and across the River Dochart (opposite)

casting for that ever-more-elusive king of river, the wild salmon.

Continue to the end of the lane to meet the busy A85, the main road through Glen Dochart. Here, at **Ledcharrie (2h15min)**, turn right and, after a short distance, take the footpath on the far side of the road, signposted 'Balquhidder'. Walk south for only about 700m to join the course of the dismantled RAILWAY, above the left bank of the **Ledcharrie Burn (2h30min)**. Turn left and follow the raised trackbed northeast (wet in places), passing over old railway bridges on the way. A tiny shed built from old railway sleepers might prove a useful shelter in bad weather, but you might well have to share it with sheep!

Walk over a long, high bridge at **Glendhu**, above the river, at the edge of the coniferous forest (**3h**). Although it is now slowly becoming obscured by trees, you will soon encounter on the left the derelict platform and ruined cottages at old **Killin Junction** STATION, beyond which the track bed forks (**3h15min**). Go right here (or, if you wish, take the shorter and more direct route back, following the Killin branch).

Heading east, the route of the railway gradually rises on a gentle gradient through the plantation. At the time of writing (1998), a felling programme was underway which is going to change the distribution of the trees, perhaps clearing the way for an unobscured views to Ben Lawers. The 'walkers welcome' signs and the occasional picnic table suggests that the recreational potential of old railways, as well as forestry plantations, is now becoming widely recognised.

At GLENOGLE COTTAGES (**4h05min**), leave the old railway and cross the A85 in **Glen Ogle**, going up to the CAR PARK

n the left. In summer, there is usually a mobile snack bar
ere for refreshments. Pursue the track past picnic tables,
kirting round the hillside at the top of the forestry plan-
tion as you enjoy the view to the mountains above Killin.

After turning right at a T-junction, climb higher and go
ver the bridge at the **Achmore Burn** (**5h**). After another
km, cross the **Allt Lochan nan Geadas** and descend to a
ll TRANSMITTER (**5h30min**). Follow the tarmac track down
hrough forestry to join the public road. Turn left and
ollow this quiet road back into Killin (**6h10min**).

9 GLEN LYON

See photograph page 24　　　　　**Distance:** 22km/13.5mi; 5h05m

Grade: a moderate but long walk, with no steep climbs, following clearly-defined track in one direction and a tarred lane in the other

Equipment: no special equipment necessary, but 3-season walkin boots recommended. OS Landranger sheet 51

How to get there and return: 🚗 Park near the post office at Bridge Balgie in Glen Lyon (Car tour 3). *No public transport.* Nearest a commodation at Invervar Lodge in Glen Lyon or at Fortingall or Killi

Shorter walks: The walk splits well into two halves. Having reache Balnahanaid, you can cross the bridge to Camusvrachan for the roa back to Bridge of Balgie (12.5km/8mi; 3h10min). Alternatively, walk ju the Camusuruchan to Invervar section and back (11km/7mi; 2h50mir

Longer walks: From the Gleann Dà-Eig, continue south on the track the top of the glen. From there, walk down to the roadside cairn ne Lochan na Larige and follow the road down to Bridge of Balg (16km/10mi; 5h10min). For another good, long alternative, follow th track and path through the Lairig Ghallabhaich to reach Loch Rannoc and the marvellous Black Wood (Caledonian Forest), beginning Innerwick and returning the same way (20km/12.5mi; 5h30min).

Postcards of Glen Lyon confidently echo the assertior of locals, that theirs is 'Scotland's most beautiful glen It is indeed a peaceful, lush and fertile haven, beautifu albeit in a tame and rustic sort of way — very differen for instance, from the dramatic and solemn beauty of th much more popular Glen Coe. At 48km/30mi from en to end, Glen Lyon is considered Scotland's longest. Th walk covers only a small part of it — to my mind the mos scenically varied and picturesque section.

Begin the walk from the BRIDGE OF BALGIE, crossing t the south side of the river and soon turning left on a trac signposted 'Meggernie Outdoor Centre'. Pause to visit secluded CEMETERY within a small walled enclosure on th left (**10min**), with a baptismal font near the entrance.

Beyond the outdoor centre, continue east, climbing ladder STILE at the edge of a birch wood, next to the **Rive Lyon**. Follow the line of a ruined wall on the left, enjoyin all the while the magnificence of the scenery around you At the farm at **Roroyere** (**50min**), take the track going u the right side of the **Allt Gleann Dà-Eig**. Higher up quickly becomes less defined and grassy, then narrows t

path. You will notice there is a much better track on the ast side of the burn, but it is not nearly as attractive.

It is well worth exploring the scattered remains of 17th- nd 18th-century dwellings on the hillside up here. The uined walls of cottages are all that is now left of a village nd a time when this glen, as other highland areas, would ave been far more populated. Some still have their owan trees growing beside them, originally planted to rotect inhabitants against witches.

Higher up the hill and a further 500m or so beyond the uins, cross the burn on your left. A convenient place to o so is where a DRYSTONE WALL, running west to east, issects the burn (**1h25min**). On the far side, join the etter track and walk downhill, to join the main track at alnahanaid (**1h45min**) and turn right. As you head back own into Glen Lyon, the view east is wonderful.

You will pass in front of a new house at **Roromore**, ollowed by the farm, before the track becomes more vergrown on entering a hazel copse. The River Lyon is lose by and the prettiness of the scenery never fades, ven when in the vicinity of the plantations that partially lanket the hill slopes on both sides.

A humpback bridge takes you across the **Inverinain urn** (**2h40min**), and some way after that the rough track nds on joining a much better one, at the edge of attrac- ive deciduous woods. Go left and down over a sturdy ridge across the river to reach the tarmac lane (**3h 0min**). Invervar Lodge is opposite and offers good B&B ccommodation. They have a very friendly cat too.

The return trip follows the quiet little lane back through he glen, this time on the north side of the river. At **Inner- vick** (**4h50min**) there is a lovely little church, a war memorial, and picnic tables. Back at the BRIDGE OF BALGIE, ou can peruse landscape paintings depicting local scenes t a gallery off the road on the right. Then stop at the post ffice (**5h05min**) for a welcome cup of tea with cakes.

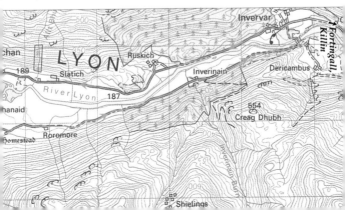

10 BEN LAWERS

See also photograph page 25 **Distance:** 10.5km/6.5mi; 5

Grade: a strenuous walk involving an ascent of 885m/2900ft on a well worn path; no technical difficulty. Competence with a compass advisable (see notes on 'Walking').

Equipment: 3- or 4-season walking boots and wind/waterproofs recommended. OS Landranger sheet 51

How to get there and return: 🚗 Park at the National Trust Visitor Centre car park on Ben Lawers (Car tour 3). 🚐 Postbus from Killin or Kenmore can drop you off/collect you at Edramucky at the bottom of the Ben Lawers road, 3km/2mi south of the Visitor Centre. Nearest accommodation is at Killin.

Shorter walks: You can climb only to Beinn Ghlas and return same way (8km/5mi; 3h40min), although the best views are from higher up. Meall nan Tarmachan, detached from the Lawers range, is at the east end of a fine undulating ridge and offers a very different alternative. Walk up its broad south ridge from the track below the summit; this track starts just north of the Visitor Centre. Return the same way (8.5km/5.3mi; 3h30min).

Longer walks: It is feasible to include any of the five neighbouring Munros of the Lawers range for a particularly challenging day.

The ascent of Ben Lawers is, for many reasons, one of the most popular hillwalks in Scotland. Apart from being the highest mountain in the Southern Highlands and an exceptional viewpoint, Ben Lawers is easily reached from Glasgow, Edinburgh, Stirling or Perth. It has a well-defined path leading to the summit from a point more than a third of the way up the mountain. Also, because of a unique combination of calcareous soils, climate, topography and altitude, the mountain harbours some very rare flora. There are alpine flowers found nowhere else in Britain. The Visitor Centre has a plethora of information on hand to offer budding botanists.

Begin the walk at the CAR PARK, crossing the boardwalk over the water-logged ground. The plants growing here are typical of upland bog areas and include bogmoss, bog asphodel and cotton-grass as well as insectivorous sundew and butterwort, both of which spread sticky leaves to catch insects, which provide essential nitrogen-containing nutrients.

Approaching Ben Lawers from Beinn Ghlas, in winter

76

Cross the ladder STILE (**5min**) which gives access to the enclosure around the **Edramucky Burn**. The fencing is necessary to restore vegetation and help reinstate a range of plants by removing grazing. Notice the difference (the fence-line effect) in the maturity and the diversity of the plants growing on the inside of the enclosure, compared to the impoverished grassland on the open hillside which continues to be intensively grazed by blackface sheep. To lessen the impact of trampling, FOLLOW THE SIGNS through the reserve which keep you on the path yet still allow you to enjoy the unique summertime flora, including alpine forget-me-not, alpine saxifrage, rock speedwell and alpine lady's mantle.

At the top of the reserve you may notice the ruins of two *shielings* (small summertime dwellings used by 17th- and 18th-century graziers). From near here, go over a second STILE (**40min**), to gain the footpath to Ben Lawers. A path on the left ascends Coire Odhar but, instead, continue up the steep grassy slope leading onto the CREST of an obvious ridge (**1h20min**). Footpath erosion has become a serious problem on Ben Lawers, testimony to the vast numbers of walkers who climb the mountain. A programme of footpath maintenance is under way to create a more stable surface.

The ridge leading up to Beinn Ghlas is steeper still, but marked by cairns and easily followed. Other than the hazard of loose rocks, easily dislodged after the spring

thaw, th
climb presen
no difficulty. Th
summit of th
Munro lies abo
100m northeast
the last of the cairn
The TOP OF **Beinn Ghla**
(**2h**) is a particularly fir
perch, from where Be
Lawers attains an attracti
pyramidal form, but be ale
to the precipitous drop on th
north side of the mountain.

From Beinn Ghlas, follow th
path down to an obvious co
(**2h20min**), before striking off up t
your next summit. After a gruellir
final 200m of ascent you reach the tr
pillar at the TOP OF **Ben Lawers** (**2**
40min). What a view! The magnificent panorama
entirely befitting of its height: on a clear day, th
Cairngorm plateau is visible, as is Ben Nevis and mar
of the Argyll mountains. Indeed, many of the mountair
highlighted in Car tours 2, 3 and 4, with their associate
walks, can be seen. In contrast to this view, beyond Loc
Tay to the east, lie the flatter fertile lowlands of Perthshire

At 1214m/3,983ft, Ben Lawers falls just short of beir
included in the exclusive 'Scottish Fours' list (mountai
over 4000ft). To rectify this, some years ago, enthusias
constructed a 6m/20ft-high tower on its summit. Toda
a pile of rubble is all that remains, a sad memorial to
failed attempt at deceiving nature! But for me, Ben Lawe
will always be special for my experience of that rar
phenomenon of the mountains, the 'Brocken spectre
This almost supernatural vision, observing your ow
shadow projected onto a bank of cloud and encircled b
'glories' (haloes) of rainbows, is caused by a very rar
combination of climatic conditions: a low sun to one sid
of you, with cloud or mist below you on the other side.

Descend Ben Lawers by retracing your steps via Beir
Ghlas, to return to the VISITOR CENTRE (**5h**).

1 BEN NEVIS

Distance: 13km/8mi; 6h

Grade: a very strenuous walk up the 'pony track', involving an ascent and corresponding descent of 1340m/4400ft. The footpath is clearly defined throughout, and there is no technical difficulty. Avoid the summit if cloud-covered and especially in white-out conditions. Competence with a compass is *essential* (see notes on 'Walking').

Equipment: 3- or 4-season walking boots, wind/waterproofs, spare layers and extra warm clothing. The mountain is notorious for sudden changes in weather conditions and temperatures. OS Landranger sheet 41

How to get there and return: 🚗 Park by the side of the road near the YH at Glen Nevis (Car tour 4). 🚌 Gaelic Bus runs a service from Fort William to/from Glen Nevis four times daily (Easter to end of October only). Nearest accommodation is Glen Nevis YH, with other B&B accommodation in the glen and at Fort William.

Alternative walks: When Ben Nevis is covered in cloud, the Mamores range, on the south side of Glen Nevis, offers fabulous alternatives. Many of the walks to these peaks begin at Polldubh or near Steall Waterfall.

By European standards, Ben Nevis is not a big mountain but, by virtue of being Britain's highest, it is a huge magnet for walkers. The main 'tourist' path, or 'pony track', up the west side of the mountain is easy to follow. This ascent involves no technical difficulty and whilst children frequently make it to the top in trainers, such indifference is not to be recommended. There are more fatalities on Ben Nevis than on any other mountain in Britain, although it is true that most accidents befall over-ambitious rock climbers scaling cliffs on the mountain's northeast face. However, the potential for serious hazards, on a summit obscured by cloud nine days in every ten and which records an average mean temperature of just below freezing, is very real indeed. Do not be deceived by a clear sunny day in Fort William. Always carry plenty of warm clothing and be prepared to make a hasty retreat if conditions on the mountain deteriorate. *Never underestimate Ben Nevis.*

Start the walk from the FOOTBRIDGE, near the youth hostel. The path begins from the east bank of the **River Nevis**, where there is an INFORMATION BOARD and also usually a WEATHER FORECAST for the day. Climb the well-engineered path which rises steeply to meet the 'PONY TRACK' (**20min**) from Achintee Farm, after about 150m of

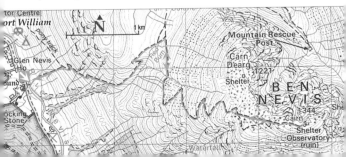

ascent. Turn right, continuing the climb. It is difficult to loose your way on such a clearly-defined path. A programme of path repair is helping to keep a check on the damage from so many feet; do adhere to requested diversions to prevent unnecessary erosion. In the 1920 this path was actually wide and stable enough to allow a model T-Ford to be driven to the summit as a publicity stunt!

Glen Nevis from the Ben Nevis 'tourist path'

The gradient eases at about 600m altitude. Walk across the spongy ground here, at the top of the gully cut by **Red Burn**. At a large CAIRN (**1h25min**), turn right and simply follow the seemingly endless series of zigzags going up the mountainside. It is a rather monotonous slog until, at last, you reach the edge of the vast summit plateau (**3h05min**), a 36 ha (90 acre) boulder field. A gentle ascent from here on leads to the trig pillar on top of a large cairn, adjacent to the emergency shelter at the SUMMIT OF **Ben Nevis** (**3h30min**).

Having reached the summit, you have every right to savour a tremendous feeling of achievement. Your reward, as you might expect standing on the roof of Britain, is a vista beyond comparison on these islands. On an exceptionally clear day one can make out the coast of Northern Ireland, but should the view of such a distant land elude you, then at least the principle mountain ranges of the Highlands should not — among them the Cairngorms, the Torridons, and the Skye Cuillin. The Mamores, Glen Coe and the Argyll mountains can be seen to the south.

But there are also features of interest up here on the summit plateau itself, most notably the crumbling ruins of an old observatory. On a more sombre note, you can read the dedications at the various memorial cairns, some paying tribute to the victims of war, others commemorating the casualties of the mountain. It is as well to be aware that the main hazard for walkers has proved to be the 600m drop from the top of the cliffs, the edge of which is just metres from the summit cairn and almost completely invisible in a white-out! Sharing the joys of the summit with other walkers is inevitable. It is rather sad however that evidence to the mountain's popularity is manifest in the form of crisp packets, tin cans and broken glass. Ben Nevis is Britain's loftiest rubbish tip!

Go back the same way to return to **Glen Nevis** (**6h**).

12 NEVIS GORGE

Distance: 6km/3.7mi; 1h30min

Grade: a short, easy walk on a popular path that is rough in places

Equipment: no special equipment necessary, but 3-season walking boots are recommended. OS Landranger sheet 41

How to get there and return: 🚗 Park at the car park at the top of the Glen Nevis road (Car tour 4). 🚌 For bus service and accommodation in Glen Nevis, see Walk 11, page 79, but note that the bus goes only as far as the YH below Ben Nevis, 6km from the start of this walk.

Longer walks: A good path beyond Steall Bridge gives access to the uppermost reaches of Glen Nevis; follow it as far as you like before returning. Very keen walkers can embark on a marathon trek all the way to the YH at Loch Ossian (25.7km/16mi; 10h30min), returning the next day or catching the train back to Fort William from the remote station at Corrour.

The unique Nevis Gorge has been described as being Himalayan in character. Here, the Water of Nevis accelerates to a fast and furious pace, forcing a way through a tortuous gap in the rocks. This narrowest of defiles marks the abrupt boundary between Britain's highest mountain and the Mamores range. The gorge is the spectacular highlight of Glen Nevis. Above the car park, at the end of the Glen Nevis road, a long cascade of water can be seen coming down from Ben Nevis.

Begin this short walk at the CAR PARK: take the footpath going east, signposted 'PUBIC FOOTPATH TO CORROUR 15 AND RANNOCH 25'. This well-trodden path penetrates the gorge on a route high above the river. You will quickly enter thick woodland, where birch, hazel, Scots pine and rowan trees somehow manage to cling to the sides of the precipice. Where the path forks, go left in the direction of a YELLOW ARROW (**10min**). Soon after, cross the **Allt Garbh** at a footbridge (**15min**) and from here continue south.

At a gap between the screen of trees on your right, there is an opportunity to look back down through the glen before the sides of the gorge are squeezed to a bottleneck. Take special care from where the path turns rough underfoot, cautiously making your way over the protruding roots and exposed, wet rocks. Before too long, the river below you is a rampant torrent, bursting out in fierce cauldrons between a chaos of fallen boulders. In places, the force of the water has behaved as if it were nature's very own sculptor, boring holes through solid rock, smoothing them down to weird and sensual shapes. Then, suddenly, you are released from the confines of the gorge and let loose out onto an OPEN MEADOW (**25min**; Picnic 4).

With a magnificent surrounding of dramatic mountain slopes, together with the plunge of the Steall Waterfall as a backdrop, the river here sings a very different tune. All is tranquil, the water meandering peacefully across a grassy plain.

Proceed along the path by the left side of the meadow, coming as close as you can get to the silvery cascade that is **Steall Waterfall** (**35min**). The water — the third highest waterfall in Scotland — plunges down a rock face for 100m/330ft, from probably one of the finest examples of a hanging valley that you would see anywhere.

Most visitors go no further than this point. However, it is rewarding to follow the path beside the Water of Nevis for another 800m/half a mile, to the bridge over the **Allt Coire Giubhsachan** (**45min**). The unique topography of the area can be fully appreciated from here. Before turning back, you might also wish to examine the ruins at **Steall**.

Retracing earlier footsteps to the CAR PARK (**1h30min**) completes this short walk. However, for a fun-filled distraction on your way back, why not dare your companions to run the gauntlet of the Steall 'high wire act', a bridge that is merely three suspended cables (one to walk on and two to hold on to) above the river!

Steall Waterfall in Glen Nevis (Picnic 4)

13 THE LOST VALLEY

Distance: 5km/3.1mi; 2h10min

Grade: a short, easy-moderate walk involving a relatively sharp ascent of 230m/754ft on a rough path through a boulder-strewn valley

Equipment: 3- or 4-season walking boots should be worn, and it is a good idea to be prepared for changes in the mountain weather but no other equipment is necessary. OS Landranger sheet 41

How to get there and return: 🚗 Park at either of two car parks situated just west of the cottage at Allt-na-reigh in Glen Coe (Car tour 4). 🚌 Scheduled coaches and buses are unlikely to stop for you in the Pass of Glencoe, but the Glencoe to Glen Etive Postbus will do so. Nearest accommodation is at the Clachaig Inn or in Glencoe village.

Longer walks: The possibilities for both high- and low-level walks are endless. The fabulous array of peaks and ridges above Glen Coe all have challenging routes of ascent, with the mountains above the Coire Gabhail being the highest of them all. From the turning-back point in Walk 13, you could continue southwest up the steep wall at the head of the corrie, onto the ridge. Then turn right for the summit of Bidean nam Bian. Return via Stob Coire nan Lochan (10km/6.2mi; 6h). A fine low-level walk would be to explore the Lairig Eilde and Lairig Gartain in a circuit around the Buachaille Etive Beag (13.4km/8.5mi; 6h), beginning from The Study or at Dalness.

It is hard to imagine a more dramatic and secluded setting than the Coire Gabhail, surrounded as it is by the towering peaks of Bidean nam Bian, Argyll's highest mountain. Here, the unruly MacDonalds used to hide their stolen cattle, confident that they would remain undiscovered; this is presumably how the corrie became known as The Lost Valley. The true magnificence of the place is best realised by climbing up to the flat mouth of the corrie, a mountain sanctuary hidden from the Pass of Glencoe.

Begin the walk from one of the two large CAR PARKS beside the A82 in Glen Coe, west of the cottage at Allt-na-reigh. (In summer you can *hear* exactly where to park. For the benefit of foreign tourists who arrive by the coach-

Glen Coe: the Lost Valley

load, tartan-clad pipers gather at the car parks to play the same tired old tunes. But then audible discord and reinforcing the highland myth has never got in the way of selling Scotland!) Escape the noise by walking down to meet the footpath below the road.

Follow the path all the way down to the footbridge over the **River Coe** (**15min**) and climb up through the birch scrub on the south side. There is a ladder STILE (**25min**) over fencing at the top of an enclosure. The trees within are slowly regenerating, being spared the ravages of grazing. The stream on your left tumbles by in a series of lovely cascades through the narrow defile between Beinn Fhada and Gearr Aonach. With Aonach Dubh, the three mountains rise in near-vertical fashion, appearing above Glen Coe as huge daunting buttresses of bare rock and known collectively as **The Three Sisters**.

Wood anemones, bluebells and primroses are among the flowers that bring splashes of springtime colour to the woodland which cloaks the bank-side. The path weaves between a jumble of boulders and having stepped across the stream, the **Allt Coire Gabhail** (**45min**), climbs to the top of the wood. The gradient eases off and then suddenly, on reaching the lip of the **Coire Gabhail** (**55min**), a flat boulder-strewn corrie floor stretches out in front of you. Surrounded by an impressive skyline of peaks, the corrie is a quiet and secluded sanctuary, a setting that has been described as an Alpine cirque.

Adventurous campers will find the grassy floor perfect for putting up a tent, while scramblers can exercise on the huge boulders scattered around. Walk on a little further if you wish to explore the deeper recesses of the corrie floor; perhaps you might even discover just where the stream, the Allt Coire Gabhail, has disappeared to! But above all The Lost Valley is a place for ponderers; it deserves a contemplative approach.

Head back to the main road in Glen Coe, following the Allt Coire Gabhail downstream by the same path (**2h10min**).

85

14 PAP OF GLENCOE

Distance: 7.7km/4.8mi; 3h

Grade: a moderate-strenuous walk involving a steep climb of 725m/2378ft up a rough path, with some light scrambling near the summit. Competence with a compass is advisable (see notes on 'Walking').

Equipment: 3- or 4-season walking boots and wind/waterproofs. OS Landranger sheet 41

How to get there and return: 🚗 Park in Glencoe village at the Bridge of Coe (Car tour 4). 🚌 Served by Fort William to Edinburgh/Glasgow scheduled coaches as well as Fort William to Glen Etive Postbus. Nearest accommodation in Glencoe village.

Shorter walk: There are Forestry Commission trails in the woods around 'Hospital Lochan' — choose your own easy walk from a combination of colour-coded waymarked walks (up to 2h).

Longer walk: For this strenuous circuit, leave your car at the Clachaig Inn, 3km southeast of Glencoe. Walk back along the lane to the Bridge of Coe and climb the Pap, picking up the walk below just before the house at 'Laraichean' (the 15min-point). Then continue along the ridge to Sgorr nam Fiannaidh, descending the Munro's steep south slope to Loch Achtriochtan for the return to your car (10.2km/6.3mi; 5h30min).

As a walking and climbing area, Glen Coe has an international reputation that is hard to beat. Most of the mountains which demarcate the north and south side of the glen present difficult challenges to the uninitiated. The Aonach Eagach (Notched Ridge), the toughest route of them all, is considered the finest ridge on the Scottish mainland and involves difficult scrambling all the way. Other mountains around offer slightly less daunting prospects, but perhaps the one 'easy' mountain walk in Glen Coe is that to Sgorr na Ciche (Pap or 'Breast' of Glencoe); this is a straightforward ascent giving rise to an outstanding view.

Start the walk from the parking place by the BRIDGE OF COE, following the lane southeast and upstream, close to the river, beneath the canopy of beech trees. Just after the house at 'Laraichean', go through a GATE (**15min**) at a cattle enclosure on the left. A rough track takes you northeast up the hillside for a short distance, directly towards the summit. Often there are highland cattle grazing here, but do not be alarmed. Despite their intimidating headgear, the animals are quite safe, unless you happen to come between a mother and calf!

Turn right to cross a STREAM (**20min**) and follow a rough footpath across the flank of the hill. At barely 100m up, the view is already very fine, especially looking back west. After a few more minutes, having crossed another stream, the hard work begins in earnest. Pursue the eroded but clearly visible path rising up the heather-clad hillside to your left, following the course of a tree-lined ravine. Gaining height quickly, you will undoubtedly need to catch your breath — and there is an ideal boulder 'seat' (**45min**) for just such a pause, a little way above a section of flattened sheep fencing.

The path detours briefly to the right but, further up, crosses scree at the TOP OF THE RAVINE (**1h15min**). Climb up out of the ravine easily and continue along a stony path. This soon leads up to the COL (**1h20min**) immediately below the rugged summit cone of the Pap. Ahead of you, an impressive landscape is revealed. Reaching inland, among a cradle of mountains, is Loch Leven, but the prospect from the very top is better still, so linger no longer. Bear left at the CAIRN and begin the final 150m push for the top. The path up the shattered quartzite of the rugged cone is steep and hard going but involves no more than a brief spell of easy scrambling to reach the TOP OF **Sgorr na Ciche** (**1h35min**). Four stone cairns in a line advertise the summit, while the **Pap**'s very highest point, at 742m/2434ft, is also marked by a pile of stones acting as a windbreak.

Although falling well short of Munro height, the Pap is nevertheless a mountain of great character, possessing a very distinctive profile which makes it recognisable from miles away. The view from the summit is

View across Loch Leven to the Pap of Glencoe, from Ballachulish

extensive, the feeling of height marvellously exaggerated by virtue of it being a vantage point directly above the sea. To the west, beyond Loch Leven and Loch Linnhe, can be seen the distant mountains of Morvern. The Mamores range and Ben Nevis are to the north.

Clamber back down to the col below and then walk over and back to the JUNCTION OF PATHS at the top of the ravine (**1h55min**). The quickest descent is to retrace your ascent route. However, you can vary this by using an alternative path that is slightly less jarring on knees. Follow the path down to the left, across the flank of the hill slope, to join a path which descends the west side of **Sgorr nam Fiannaidh** (**2h10min**). Turn right and go downhill more steeply, regaining the ascent path above the flattened SHEEP FENCING (**2h20min**) which was encountered on your ascent. From here, continue your descent to **Glencoe** over familiar ground (**3h**).

Walk 15: River Dee near Braemar, below Morrone

15 MORRONE

See photographs opposite and pages 30 and 31

Distance: 11.4km/7mi; 3h15min

Grade: a moderate walk involving straightforward ascents totalling 550m/1804ft. This relatively-safe mountain has clear paths and tracks which ensures an uninterrupted walking pace. Competence with a compass is advisable (see notes on 'Walking').

Equipment: 3- or 4-season walking boots and wind/waterproofs. OS Landranger sheet 43

How to get there and return: 🚗 Park in Braemar (Car tour 5). 🚌 Regular coach connection with Aberdeen and Ballater; also on Ballater to Linn of Dee Postbus route. Nearest accommodation in Braemar.

Shorter walks: Follow the main walk up to the view indicator at Tomintoul and return same way (2.8km/1.8mi; 40min) or explore the Morrone Birchwood at will.

Longer walk: Where the descent track veers east, approximately 1.5km/1mi south of Morrone's summit, go west into Coire nam Freumh and descend to the Linn of Corriemulzie, following the path beside the burn of the same name. Then follow the minor road above the River Dee northeast back to Braemar (14km/8.7mi; 4h15min), or use NNR tracks and paths.

> 'Upon this vantage ground I fain would stand
> A prospect with delight my spirit fills
> How oft in glowing rapture have I scanned
> the waving outline of the distant hills.'
>   George Steven (Deeside poet)

Morrone, or Morven, rises prominently above Braemar. Rounded in profile and bereft of sharp ridges or steep-sided corries or rocky pinnacles, it epitomises the apparently featureless character of the Grampian Mountains. Nevertheless, its summit is an exceptionally fine viewpoint, a prize well within the capabilities of the modest hillwalker. Furthermore, the unique Morrone Birchwood is just a short walk south of Braemar. Considered the finest example of upland birchwood in Great Britain, budding botanists will find reasons to linger on the lime-rich slopes among juniper, wild thyme and mountain flowers including alpine cinquefoil.

Start the walk at the BRAEMAR GALLERY. Walk west along the road, then go left (signposted 'Forest Walk and Duckpond 1/2m).' Just past the DUCK POND (**10min**), take the track to the right, signposted 'Morrone and Birchwood'. Go left where the track divides, then right at a cottage, continuing uphill to where the track forks again. Here, take the left-hand track, to a bench and VIEW INDICATOR (**20min**). Even if you venture no further, you will at least enjoy a fine view of the Cairngorms in return for very little effort — such are the advantages of starting the walk from a village over 300m/1000ft above sea level.

To the right of a NNR sign, gain the well-worn path marked 'Morrone', walking up through the heather. Go through a KISSING-GATE (**35min**) from where, looking back, the Dee valley and Braemar are well seen. CAIRNS mark the straightforward route over ground where, on this north side of the mountain, snow pockets are prone to linger. When the TRANSMISSION MASTS ahead of you come into view, head straight towards them across an otherwise rather bleak and featureless slope. At the SUMMIT OF **Morrone** (**1h25min**) there is a trig pillar and a large cairn, adjacent to the main mast, from where the view of the Cairngorms across the Dee valley is outstanding.

Continue the walk using the landrover track on the south side of the mountain, initially coming to an indistinct SECOND SUMMIT (**1h45min**). From here veer east and stay on the track for a fast descent to **Glen Clunie** (**2h 25min**). Turn left at the bottom and follow the minor road north, beside **Clunie Water**. The A93 is never far away, but it is a lovely walk through the valley to Braemar. At the GOLF COURSE (**2h50min**), a footbridge over the river gives access to the YH and the houses on the main road at the south end of the village. Alternatively, continue on to Braemar and the BRIDGE over Clunie Water (**3h15min**).

16 LOCHNAGER

Distance: 18km/11.2mi; 6h

Grade: a long and strenuous walk involving 800m/2624ft of gradual ascent, but on mostly good paths, with just one steep section. Competence with a compass is *essential* (see notes on 'Walking').

Equipment: 3- or 4-season walking boots, wind/waterproofs and spare layers. OS Landranger sheet 44

How to get there and return: 🚗 Park in the large car park at the Spittal of Glenmuick (Car tour 5). No public transport in Glen Muick. 🚌 Coach services to Ballater (12km north-northeast) from Aberdeen and Braemar. Nearest accommodation in Ballater, Deeside.

The summit of Lochnager from the north slope

Shorter walk: Follow the main walk to the col below Meikle Pap, for a fine view of Lochnager's famous northeast corrie (12km/7.5mi; 3h45min). Any exploration of Loch Muick from the 'Spittal' car park is rewarding and involves no climbing.

Longer walk: Returning from Lochnager by the path down the Glas Allt to Loch Muick provides an enjoyable alternative return (20km/12.5mi; 6h45min).

'O for the rocks that are wild and majestic
the steep frowning glories of dark Lochnagar'
(Byron)

The Grampian Mountains, along with many of those on the eastern side of Scotland, tend to conceal their charms. Characterised by vast, high, featureless plateaux, you have to get intimate with them to see them at their best. But Lochnager, the high and conspicuous peak on the northern escarpment of the White Mount tableland, is the notable exception. It is the highest point of a great wedge of granite that towers above Deeside and which harbours probably the finest corrie of the Grampians, much celebrated by royalty as well as artists and poets. The easiest and by far the most popular walking route to the summit of the mountain begins from Glen Muick.

Start the walk from the large CAR PARK at the Spittal of Glenmuick. Beyond the picnic tables, go past the modest Visitor Centre amongst the pines, gaining the track which soon crosses the **River Muick** at a timber bridge (**10min**). Continue to **Allt na-giubhsaich** (**20min**), where you should then take the rough path which passes in front of an uninhabited house. Beyond the pines, join a track that climbs gradually west over the open moorland, beside a burn that is later easily crossed (**35min**).

Make your way ever higher over the heather-carpeted moorland, the track climbing above the steep-sided ravine where the stream begins its life (**55min**). You will reach a CAIRN (**1h10min**) at the next junction of paths. Here, take the well-maintained and easy-to-follow path on the left, going west. Higher up and located a few metres to the left of the path, you can visit the MEMORIAL STONE (**1h40min**) marked on the map.

Look out for that high-rise chameleon of the bird world, the ptarmigan, the sight of which is as good an indication as any that you are more than 750m/2500ft above sea level. The plumage of these birds, adapted to

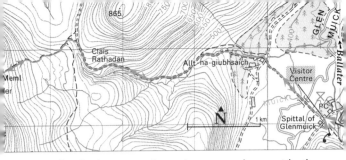

life on the high mountains, changes colour with the seasons and is dependant on the degree of snow cover; they are not always easy to spot.

On regaining the path and climbing higher, you will soon arrive at the COL (**2h**) immediately south of **Meikle Pap**. Here, at the edge of the corrie, you can now take in the awe-inspiring scenery in front of you. The precipitous escarpment of granite cliffs which surrounds the dark waters of the loch is a not only tremendously impressive sight, but is a favourite playground of rock climbers from Dundee. Even if you go no further, you can return having enjoyed the finest aspect of the mountain, the magnificent northeast corrie of Lochnager. In any case, if the weather has deteriorated, its is advisable not to go any higher. In clear conditions however, carry on to the summit.

Walk back 100m or so and then climb the steep slope known as **The Ladder**, staying close to the edge of the corrie on the way up. Having gained what seems the level roof of the mountain, the top of the plateau, walk west and around the rim of the corrie, to pass first the granite tor at **Cac Carn Mór** ('big shit cairn'; **3h10min**), then bear north to **Cac Carn Beag** ('little shit cairn'), the TRUE SUMMIT OF **Lochnager** (**3h20min**). There is a trig pillar at 1155m/3789ft, as well as a view indicator which helps you identify all the mountains to be seen across a panorama that extends far beyond Balmoral Forest and the Cairngorms. Looking southwards, in very clear weather, some claim it is possible to make out the Forth Bridge.

The fastest descent is made by retracing your ascent route (**6h**).

17 GLEN QUOICH

Distance: 14km/8.7mi; 3h35min

Grade: a moderate walk involving very little ascent, on mostly good paths and tracks. Two potentially problematic river crossings.

Equipment: 3- or 4-season walking boots, but no other special equipment necessary. OS Landranger sheet 43

How to get there and return: 🚗 Park on the grass by Quoich Water, at the end of the minor road at Allanaquoich (Car tour 5). 🚐 Postbus connection to Braemar. Nearest accommodation at Muir Cottage YH and at Braemar.

Shorter walks: Situated 2km/1.2mi upstream from the Linn of Quoich is a little footbridge over the river; a return by the opposite bank makes a very pleasant short walk (4.5km/2.7mi; 1h15min). Alternatively, simply walk back the same way when you have ventured far enough up the glen.

Longer walk: From Glen Quoich, go over the pass of Clais Fhearnaig and return via Glen Lui to the road near Mar Lodge (15.8km/10mi; 4h45min).

The gentle countryside immediately to the west of Braemar has plenty to satisfy those who enjoy low-level walks, pursuing routes that explore the tributaries of the Upper Dee. These rivers and streams flow through the loveliest of glens and provide the natural corridors which connect Deeside with the Cairngorm Mountains, but they are out of bounds for motorists. Fortunately however, thanks to a network of excellent paths and tracks, this is ideal country for hiking.

Carpets of purple heather blanket vast tracks of wild moorland, and rivers dance and flow between swathes of native pine in scenes which epitomise, for many, the very essence of Scotland. To see the heather at its vivid best, then be sure to visit this northwest corner of Deeside in August, sometime around the 'glorious twelfth'. Spring is the better season if a snow-dappled mountainous backdrop appeals to you. Whenever you decide to visit this area, the scenery is always inspirational, Glen Quoich being my own favourite among the Forest of Mar valleys.

Begin the walk from the VEHICLE BRIDGE at **Allanaquoich**, at the terminus of the little road from Braemar. Walk up through the pines on the path to the footbridge at the **Linn of Quoich** (**5min**). Looking down you can see where the water has eroded a great hole through a rock slab; it is known as **The Punch Bowl**, and a delightful spot it is too.

Quoich Water, Glen Quoich

From the other side of Quoich Water, follow a path up to a TRACK (**10min**) and continue walking northwest, up into **Glen Quoich**. Passing through majestic stands of native Scots pine, you will enjoy some fine views along the river and towards the mountains at the southern edge of the vast Cairngorm plateau. Beinn a' Bhuird is the impressive peak at the top of the glen.

Pass beneath a PLANTATION ENCLOSURE on your left (**1h**) and then dip down to the banks of a burn. The path off to the left (**1h10min**) connects with Glen Lui. However, stay on the track going north.

After heavy rain, the crossing of the STREAM (**1h30min**) flowing from Dubh Ghleann is likely to prove a frustrating obstacle. In such conditions, you may have to turn back but, otherwise, cross to the far side by boulder-hopping and then pick up a track going east. Follow **Quoich Water** upstream to cross the **Alltan na Beinne** (**1h45min**), a less substantial stream. Having gained the uppermost reaches of Glen Quoich, the fording of Quoich Water should be attempted on arriving at the edge of the remote PINE WOOD (**2h**). Walk upstream a little way, to find the shallowest water … although wherever you attempt the crossing, it is likely you will have to remove boots and socks.

A track from the opposite bank climbs west and then south, which means you can now return along the other side of the glen. As you walk on, there are marvellous views across the river to where you were earlier, revealing more of the Cairngorm peaks, including a glimpse of Ben Macdui (Walk 20). To the south is Lochnager (Walk 16).

This is very much grouse country. Without intending

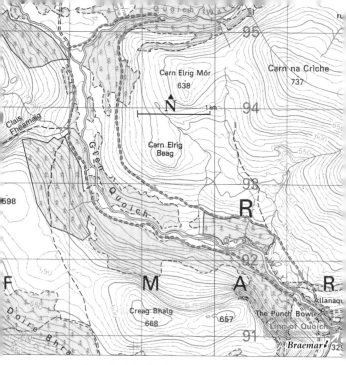

to, you will probably flush grouse from the heather, so be prepared to be startled when these large birds attempt sudden and clumsy flight from beneath you.

Your walk across the open moorland continues to the top edge of a PINE WOOD (**2h50min**). From here, dip down to cross a burn at a FOOTBRIDGE (**3h05min**) and another one at STEPPING STONES (**3h10min**). Continue your descent to the larch trees at the **Linn of Quoich**, coming from behind the cottage by the footbridge there. It is then a simple matter of wandering downstream to find your car at **Allanaquoich** again (**3h35min**).

18 ROTHIEMURCHUS AND GLEANN EINICH

Distance: 26km/16.1mi; 7h

Grade: a long and quite strenuous walk, but on good tracks and paths and with no significant gradient.

Equipment: 3- or 4-season walking boots, wind/waterproofs and food and drink. No other special equipment necessary. OS Landranger sheet 36

How to get there and return: 🚗 Park at Coylumbridge in the lay-by by Rothiemurchus Camp and Caravan Park (Car our 6). 🚌 The Aviemore/Ski Centre ous will drop you off/collect you there. Nearest accommodation is Coylumbridge Hotel, or in Aviemore.

Shorter walk: From Cairngorm Club Footbridge walk west and go around Loch an Eilein, following the nature rail, before returning via Lochan Deò 15km/9.3mi; 4h).

Longer walk: From Cairngorm Club Footbridge, continue on through the finest of Scottish mountain passes, the Lairig Ghru. This marathon trek

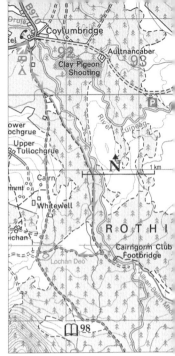

38.6km/24mi; 12h), between Coylumbridge and Braemar, is a long and hard day. The route links Speyside with Deeside and dissects the Cairngorms in a way that is not possible by car.

The Forest of Rothiemurchus is regarded as the largest and finest surviving remnant of the ancient Caledonian Forest. Less than one per cent of that original forest remains, man's insatiable timber demands having banished it from the landscape. With the exception of a few protected pockets, overgrazing by deer and sheep continues to prevent any regeneration of the forest.

Scots pines, heather, juniper and birch are flourishing at Rothiemurchus. The forest is a refuge for rare mammals and birds that have long been associated with the wildlife of Scotland and include such creatures as the wild cat, pine-marten, osprey, capercaillie and Scottish crossbill. Unlike elsewhere, red squirrels are actually quite common here, and on this walk you have a good chance of seeing them.

Start the walk on the LANDROVER TRACK skirting the right-hand edge of **Rothiemurchus** CAMP AND CARAVAN PARK, passing LAIRIG GHRU COTTAGE (**5min**). Beneath the pines, a sense of venturing into an ancient forest is exaggerated by the thick fronds of lichen which hang from many of the trees.

The track is level, dry and easy to follow. Where it divides, take the left fork towards the 'LAIRIG GHRU' passing through a series of gates before meeting another TRACK (**40min**) coming in from the right. Continue a little further to view the picturesque river, the **Allt-an-Beinn Mhòr** from the CAIRNGORM CLUB FOOTBRIDGE (**45min**). Then walk west, at first retracing your last few steps.

Having reached **Lochan Deò** at a crossroads of tracks (**1h15min**), turn left for 'LOCH EINICH'. Continuing south through the forest, you should find it easy to maintain a steady walking pace. At the bank of **Am Beanaidh**, stay on the path closest to the river. The trees are left behind after about two hours, and the left bank of the river is gained on crossing a FOOTBRIDGE (**2h 15min**).

The very dramatic kind of beauty which characterises **Gleann Einich** intensifies with every step you take, venturing ever further between constricting mountain slopes. Only the crossing of the **Beanaidh Bheag** (**2h40min**) is likely to hamper your progress — this is best attempted upstream, a little distance from the track.

Just after reaching the highest point of the walk, at 510m/1673ft (**3h25min**), the path seen on the left is one that ascends Braeriach (the third highest mountain in Britain). Instead, continue down to the north shore of Loch Einich (**3h35min**), the waters of which are cradled by huge

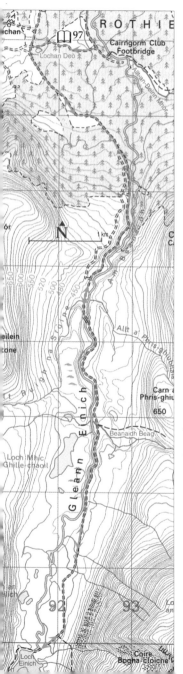

and intimidating cliffs and buttresses — a truly wild and very remote setting at the top of the glen.

Return the way you came but, for variation at the end of the walk, pursue the more direct track back. Go straight ahead at **Lochan Deò** for **Coylumbridge** (7h).

The wild, remote setting of Glen Einich, in March

19 RYVOAN PASS

Distance: 9.5km/5.9mi; 2h50min

Grade: a moderate walk involving 485m/1590ft of straightforward ascent on excellent tracks and mostly good paths. Competence with a compass is advisable (see notes on 'Walking'). Avoid Meall a Bhuachaille if it is covered in cloud, unless you are very competent with map and compass.

Equipment: 3- or 4-season walking boots and wind/waterproofs. OS Landranger sheet 36

How to get there and return: 🚗 Park by the Reindeer Centre in Glenmore Forest Park or by Loch Morlich (Car tour 6). 🚌 Local bus service connects the Cairngorm Ski Centre with Aviemore, stopping at the Reindeer Centre. Nearest accommodation is at Glenmore YH, Coylumbridge Hotel and in Aviemore.

Shorter walk: The obvious shorter walk (in time only) is to return from Ryvoan Bothy back through the Ryvoan Pass. This avoids any hillwalking (9.5km/5.9mi; 2h).

Longer walk: From Ryvoan Bothy, continue the walk north over bare moorland and descend through Abernethy Forest to Nethy Bridge (12.9km/8mi; 2h55min). From here there are coach connections back to Aviemore.

This walk falls almost entirely within the boundaries of Glenmore Forest Park, a Forestry Commission park dedicated to recreational pursuits. Pine-fringed Loch Morlich is especially popular with water sports enthusiasts. A vast maze of paths and tracks allows everyone access to an extensive swathe of attractive natural and plantation forest. Among the trees are a few hidden treasures.

Begin from REINDEER HOUSE, which is near the YH. Britain's only herd of reindeer roam free-range on the mountain slopes around here. Take the metalled track signposted to 'GLENMORE LODGE, NORWEGIAN LODGE'. Walk past GLENMORE LODGE (**15min**), the centre for a range of outdoor activities, and then follow the 'PUBLIC FOOTPATH TO FOREST LODGE AND NETHY BRIDGE', which is actually a wide gravel track.

Before very long there are Scots pines in every direction, with the forest assuming a more natural complexion on entering the **Caledonian Forest Nature Reserve** (**20min**). Blue-coded WAYMARKER

Lochan Uaine

POSTS guide the way through the **Ryvoan Pass**, an increasingly-narrow defile between crags. The beautiful old pines trees on either side hint at the character of a forested wilderness that once covered much of Scotland, but which now survives in only a few protected pockets (see Walk 18).

A remarkable little loch is soon encountered among the pines on your right, **Lochan Uaine (35min)**. It means Green Lake, a very appropriate way to describe the colour and translucence of its waters. Being a legendary home of fairies, the mystics among you might well wish to stay and make new friends!

Beyond the *lochan*, continue across a landscape now more of heather than of trees, to where the path forks. Go left here, towards 'NETHY BRIDGE' (**45min**), across the open moor and out over ground prone to becoming waterlogged in places, but still on an easily-followed path. RYVOAN BOTHY (**55min**), like other mountain bothies in Scotland, provides basic emergency accommodation only. It is in the hands of the Mountain Bothies Association to which the Bothy Code applies, as displayed inside the hut.

From the bothy there is a good view back through the Ryvoan Pass, an intimate refuge backed by the vast sweep of the Cairngorm Mountains. This is the way you should return if the prospect of climbing to the top of a mountain does not inspire you. But if you are feeling adventurous,

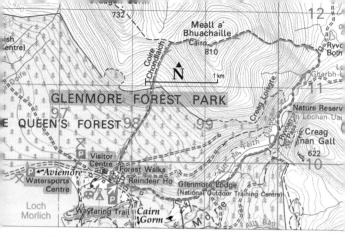

follow the rough and gradually-steepening path up the mountain slope behind the bothy, walking west. Apart from a brief steep section between boulders (**1h15min**), it is a straightforward climb all the way to the wind-swept SUMMIT OF **Meall a' Bhuachaille** (**1h50min**). It is a fantastic vantage point for appreciating the full extent of the forests of Glenmore and Rothiemurchus, as well as for absorbing the grandeur of the mountains, a sight spoiled only by the incongruous ski runs and chair lifts on Cairn Gorm. To the north lies another fine remnant of native pine, that of Abernethy Forest.

Follow a CAIRN-MARKED PATH down on the other side of the mountain and then strike off left on a wet and peaty path into the **Coire Chondlaich**. This path begins just before the lowest point of the COL (**2h05min**) and aims for Loch Morlich below. From the top edge of the **Queen's Forest** (**2h25min**), descend the left bank of the **Allt Coire Chondlaich** all the way to the forest shop and restaurant in **Glen More** (**2h50min**).

20 CAIRN GORM AND BEN MACDUI

Distance: 17.5km/10.9mi; 6h

Grade: a strenuous walk involving 980m/3214ft of ascent on mountain paths, but without technical difficulty. Perhaps more than anywhere else in the Scottish Highlands, absolute competence with a compass is *essential* on the Cairngorms (see notes on 'Walking').

Equipment: 3- or 4-season walking boots, a warm hat, wind/water-proofs, plenty of layers; set out *fully-equipped* (see notes on 'Walking'). OS Landranger sheet 36

How to get there and return: 🚗 Park in the large Coire Cas car park at the bottom of the ski pistes at Cairn Gorm (Car tour 6). 🚌 Regular bus connection with Aviemore. Nearest accommodation in Glenmore, Coylumbridge or Aviemore.

Shorter walk: Pursue the straightforward climb to Cairn Gorm as described for main walk, but use the track down from the Ptarmigan Restaurant for your return (7km/4.3mi; 3h). *On no account proceed beyond the summit in adverse weather.*

Longer walk: Return from Ben Macdui via Lurcher's Crag and the Chalamain Gap (22km/13.7mi; 7h45min).

'From the top of Ben Macdui
I shall watch the gathering storm,
And see the crisp snow lying
At the back of Cairn Gorm.
(from 'I leave tonight from Euston' by A M Lawrence)

The romance of the Cairngorms, when expressed in verse, often disguises a potentially-hostile environment. Here lies the highest land mass in Scotland, and nowhere else in Britain is there such a large tract of arctic terrain. In recognition of the importance of the rare flora and fauna of the Cairngorms, the plateau is within the boundaries of Britain's largest nature reserve.

Snow flurries can occur in July, but in good weather it is very rewarding to venture beyond Cairn Gorm itself, to the other peaks of the range. Proceeding to the summit of

Weather station on summit of Cairn Gorm in September

Cairngorm plateau, from the summit of Cairn Gorm

Ben Macdui requires an awareness of the potential hazards as well as an investment of energy, but otherwise the walk is not difficult.

Set off from the **Coire Cas** CAR PARK by striking off northeast up over the heather, staying roughly parallel to the line of ski tows. On reaching a CAIRN-MARKED route (**10min**) on the broad **An t-Aonach** ridge, turn right and follow the path rising southeast. The path, not always visible, meanders between the fencing of ski pistes. Simply pursue these to higher levels, until you reach the PTARMIGAN RESTAURANT (**1h05min**). This building is perched somewhat incongruously on the mountain at 1080m/3542ft; it is your *last chance* for coffee or food supplies.

From here follow a well-engineered path and then marker-posts up to the large cairn on the SUMMIT OF **Cairn Gorm** (**1h30min**). The weather and transmission station at the top, shown on the preceding page, frequently records the lowest temperatures in Britain! A camera linked to the Internet can relay the current situation regarding visibility and conditions. As always, real views are better than virtual ones. To look out over the plateau and along the rim of cliffs above the north-facing corries is a magnificent and awe-inspiring experience, just as you might expect from a vantage point over 1220m/4000ft above sea level.

If the weather is deteriorating or at all threatening, you should return the way you came. Otherwise, descend the bouldery slope on the west side, to reach the CAIRN (**1h50min**) at the top of the **Fiacaill a' Choire Chais**. From there, continue around the rim of the **Coire an t-Sneachda**, skirting the tops of a marvellous array of cliffs, crags and buttresses, the most impressive of which is a

jagged profile of granite known as the **Fiacaill Buttress**. At the COL (**2h30min**) just before that buttress, bear south-southwest along a path that crosses the wide, empty wilderness of the plateau.

The stony tundra under your feet supports a unique ecosystem, including rare plants normally associated with the arctic, and birds such as snow bunting and ptarmigan. It is the only place in Britain where snowy owls have been known to reside.

You will soon pass close to **Lochan Buidhe** (**2h55min**), the highest body of water in the British Isles and frozen for much of the year but, nevertheless, a welcome land-mark. Continue south across the great boulder-strewn dome, to reach the cairn on the TOP OF **Ben Macdui** (**3h40min**). At 1309m/4294ft, this Munro is second only to Ben Nevis in height. Having savoured the marvellous view, begin your descent by going back the same way. Immediately north of **Lochan Buidhe**, climb the slope to the TOP OF **Cairn Lochan** (**4h50min**), a fine summit above the north-facing corries. Then return again to the COL (**5h**) lying just east of the top of the Fiacaill Buttress.

From the col descend the head wall of the **Coire an t-Sneachda**, to reach the desolate, scree-littered *lochans*

below. From here a rough path follows the burn down-stream. Bear right near the bottom, making for the CAR PARK (**6h**) where your walk began. The more adventurous among you could always try skiing back down from Cairn Gorm, but then of course there is the chair lift!

21 FALLS OF GLOMACH

Distance: 11.3km/7mi; 4h

Grade: a moderate-strenuous walk, beginning on good forestry tracks, involving 710m/2329ft of ascent, with a steep section on a cairn-marked path leading up to high moorland.

Equipment: 3- or 4-season walking boots and wind/waterproofs, but no other special equipment necessary. OS Landranger sheet 33

How to get there and return: 🚌 Park at the Forestry Commission car park for Kintail Country Park at the end of the minor road in Strath Croe (3.5km east of the A87, at the head of Loch Duich; Car tour 7). 🚐 Postbus service from Kyle, along the A87 to/from the head of Loch Duich, 3.5km from the start of the walk. Nearest accommodation at Kintail Lodge and head of Loch Duich or Shiel Bridge.

Shorter walk: Climb Glean Choinneachain from Dorusduain, to the Bealach an Sgairne, the so-called 'Gates of Affric'. From here you can look down into upper Glen Affric (8.5km/5.3mi; 2h45min return).

Longer walk: Return to Dorusduain from the Falls of Glomach via unpathed Gleann Gaorsaic and the Bealach an Sgairne. This is a strenuous but satisfying circuit (16.5km/10.2mi; 6h).

The starting point of this walk is in Strath Croe, a river valley in the shadow of the marvellous Five Sisters of Kintail range of mountains. Their traverse is one of the finest possible ridge walks in the Scottish Highlands but a rather formidable expedition only recommended for very experienced hillwalkers. Our walk is a more modest objective, but it is a route that will give you a splendid introduction to the topography of the area, while at the same time visiting the second highest waterfall of Britain, the Falls of Glomach.

Start out on the forestry track leaving the car park, signposted 'GLOMACH FALLS 4 MILES, NO CARS PLEASE'. The track bears right as you climb gradually higher in **Dorusduain Wood**, between the regiments of conifers. Follow

further signs for 'GLOMACH FALLS' on reaching junctions with other tracks. You will pass through a number of gates between deer fencing.

Falls of Glomach

Cross a concrete bridge over the **Allt an Leòld Ghaineamhaich** (**20min**) and proceed north. It is worth scanning the skies above Beinn Bhuide and Beinn Bhreac, the high crags about 2km distant to your left, as golden eagles are frequently observed there.

On reaching the northeast corner of the plantation, go over a FOOTBRIDGE made from railway timbers (**35min**), to cross the Allt an Leòld Ghaineamhaich a second time. From the edge of the forest here, bear right and ascend the zigzagging footpath that quickly brings you above the north bank of the stream. Continue east up the left side of this grassy gorge, on a steep path of varying condition, which follows the stream to its upper reaches. You will notice an attractive WATERFALL on your right (**1h10min**), after which the gradient of the climb begins to ease a little. The going underfoot is somewhat wetter as you emerge onto the open moor, at the top of the **Bealach na Sròine** (**1h35min**). A succession of cairns guide you easily along this now more vague path skirting **Meall Dubh**.

Continuing northeast, you begin a gradual descent that becomes steeper. As you reach the banks of the **Allt a' Ghlomach** (**1h55min**), a NTS sign warns of the dangers of proceeding beyond the top of the falls, but it is really quite safe to proceed just a little bit further. By dropping down a few metres from the top, on the left side of the **Falls of Glomach** (**2h**), you are able to look back and view this long vertical plunge of water at its most impressive.

Return to Dorusduain Wood (**4h**) by retracing your footsteps back over the pass, the **Bealach na Sròine**.

22 BEINN SGRITHEALL

See photographs pages 34 and 36   **Distance:** 9.8km/6.1mi; 5h

Grade: a very strenuous walk, with a steep ascent of 1050m/3444ft traversing wild terrain, with a brief exposed section of high ridge. No technical difficulty, but competence with a compass is advisable (see notes on 'Walking').

Equipment: 3- or 4-season walking boots and wind/waterproofs. OS Landranger sheet 33

How to get there and return: 🚗 Park by the side of the road, by the shore of Loch Hourn at Arnisdale (Car tour 7). 🚌 Served by the Kyle/Arnisdale Postbus. Nearest accommodation at Glenelg.

Shorter walks: From the very end of the road at the hamlet of Corran, you have a choice of two short walks. One goes east and explores Glen Arnisdale by paths and tracks beside the river. Another path follows the coast southwest beside the rocky shore of Loch Hourn. In both cases, just turn around and walk back again when you have had enough.

Beinn Sgritheall rises in one great wedge, sweeping up from the shores of Loch Hourn. Out on its own, on the wild coast, it feels as remote from civilisation as it is detached from other mountains. First impressions suggest that the mountain does not actually want to be climbed, offering few obvious routes of ascent, although a relatively straightforward passage up to its ridge does exist. Once there, you will savour views that are among the best in Scotland, perhaps precisely because of its isolation. It is important to save Beinn Sgritheall for a clear day.

Begin the walk at the beautiful village of **Arnisdale**. A rudimentary sign next to a cottage points the way 'TO BEINN SGRITHEALL', by a path which follows the most westerly of the burns behind the village. Cross this water where a line of deer fencing ends and then bear right over the wet ground to cross another burn (**12min**). Follow a path of increasing steepness up the right bank of this more substantial stream, enjoying the simple pleasure of some lovely little waterfalls on the way up.

For a while, it might well seem a bit of an slog, but the climb is not difficult and there is plenty in nature to enjoy. If you are here in early summer, you may notice tiny purple flowers growing on the waterlogged ground. This is butterwort, an insectivorous plant whose sticky, star-shaped arrangement of leaves is a deadly trap for midges.

By keeping to the path you will also be following a line of old rusty sheep-fencing as far as the upper-most reaches of the stream. Cross this again (**55min**) and from the left bank continue your ascent following further rusty posts up to the pass of **Bealach Arnasdail** (**1h20min**), marked by an old rusty gate, serving no apparent purpose! If low cloud has descended, turn back now. Other-

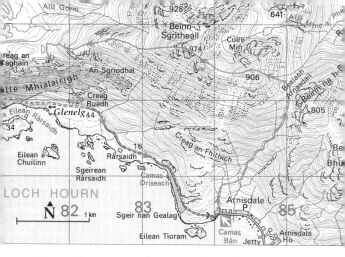

wise, walk west-northwest, at first following yet more redundant fence posts up the mountain side. Higher up you will gain a more defined path which leads to the EAST SUMMIT (**2h05min**). From here follow the clearly-defined ridge for 1km around the rim of the **Coire Min** — a very pleasant and quite unusual walk, high above the sea. There is just one narrow and quite exposed section which may cause concern if you do not have a head for heights. From the MAIN (WEST) SUMMIT OF **Beinn Sgritheall** (**2h 35min**), a tremendous view extends across Loch Hourn to the remote Knoydart mountains and out to sea to the islands of Skye and Rum. The large stone wall windbreak which has evolved on the top of this Munro could well prove useful, unlike the crumpled concrete trig pillar.

Begin your descent by continuing west. At first the path traverses a steep rocky slope, but it soon turns softer underfoot and the gradient becomes less severe. On reaching the COL at 365m/1197ft (**3h40min**), keep a look out for a TINY CAIRN on the left. If you reach a line of deer fencing or the waters of a tiny *lochan,* you have gone too far! Bear left at this cairn and descend to cross a ladder STILE (**3h45min**) at the top of a woodland area.

Continue southeast on the path, beneath majestic oaks and birch trees, where protection from grazing has allowed natural regeneration and a luxuriant ground layer has become established. In springtime all the flowers commonly associated with deciduous woodland can be found here, as can a few rarities such as marsh orchids.

The path eventually deposits you at the road below the trees of **Coille Mhialairigh** (**4h15min**). Turn left for a final 3km hike along this quiet stretch of tarmac, beside **Loch Hourn**, to reach **Arnisdale** (**5h**).

23 THE STORR

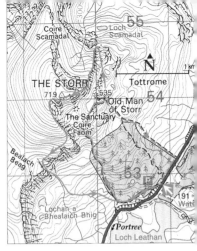

Distance: 7km/4.3mi; 3h15min

Grade: a fairly strenuous walk, involving an ascent of 555m/ 1820ft; steep in places, with difficult terrain, but no scary bits. Competence with a compass is advisable if venturing onto Trotternish Ridge (see notes on 'Walking').

Equipment: 3- or 4-season walking boots and wind/water-proofs. OS Landranger sheet 23

How to get there and return: 🚗 Park at the FC car park immediately north of Loch Leathan, 11.3km/7mi north of Portree (Car tour 8). 🚌 Local bus serves Trotternish Peninsula in a circuit from Portree. Nearest accommodation at Portree.

Shorter walks: Having reached The Old Man, the main walk is easily shortened by returning either by your ascent route or down the north side of the plantation (4.5km/2.8mi; 2h). Another short walk visits Bearreraig Bay, following a track heading east to the coast and then a path descending beside hydroelectric pipes to the fossil beach (3.8km/ 2.4mi; 1h30min).

Longer walks: From the summit of The Storr, you can venture many miles further, heading either north or south along the marvellous Trotternish Ridge.

An almost continuous line of basalt cliffs forms the steep escarpment of the Trotternish Ridge on Skye. It is a dramatic landscape when seen from the road below; spectacular when explored at close quarters. While the two-day trek along the crest of the entire ridge is considered one of the best high-level routes in Scotland, there are plenty of less challenging shorter walks amidst the intriguing landslips and isolated pinnacles of Trotternish. The Storr is the highest summit on the ridge, but it is the remarkable pillar of rock below it, known as The Old Man of Storr, which attracts far more curiosity. This walk visits both.

Begin the walk at the CAR PARK just north of Loch Leathan. First, walk back along the road and go through a KISSING GATE (**10min**) on the right, just beyond a house. From here ascend a clearly-defined grassy path up along the edge of the plantation. It may well be necessary to weave a diversion around a few spruce trees to avoid the waterlogged ground.

At the uppermost reaches of the forested area (**35min**), gain a path which continues upward more steeply. Bear right as you approach the area below the summit cliffs

(**The Sanctuary**; **50min**), and begin to venture at will along any of the tangle of paths among the weird rock formations. It is a wonderful landscape in which **The Old Man** (**1h10min**) is the most conspicuous feature, a precariously poised 50m/165ft-high pear-shaped splinter of rock. The Old Man seems almost to defy gravity, teetering as he does on an undercut plinth of bedrock. A neighbouring monolith comes complete with sharp fangs and a rock window!

The tranquillity of The Sanctuary affects all those who

The Sanctuary of The Storr and The Old Man (centre pinnacle)

linger a while. I can recall one especially poignant spring-time visit up here, totally enraptured by the echoes of ring ouzels calling to one another from one crumbling vol-canic spire to another — a mesmerising performance in the most eerie of nature's arenas.

Leaving The Sanctuary, climb higher as you go north, following the line of cliffs. You will cross some low fencing at a rudimentary STILE (**1h25min**), before turning south and climbing to the top of the **Coire Scamadal**. Stay over to the left edge as you do so, negotiating rocky outcrops with ease and passing around two obvious clefts at the cliff edge. A seemingly impregnable wall of rock then confronts you, but this is easily breached. Bear right, and walk along the inside of it for about 100m and then climb up a grassy bank to reach a small CAIRN. The trig pillar, sitting on a wide flat summit, is just a short walk away.

The SUMMIT OF **The Storr** (**2h05min**) is 719m/2358ft above sea level. From here you are able to look down and along the entire backbone of the Trotternish Peninsula, viewing the line of the escarpment cliffs in both direc-tions. The Storr is the highest point of a 32km/20mi-long ridge from where you can also savour a fine prospect of the Cuillin and much of the rest of Skye, the island of Raasay and far beyond.

On leaving the summit, stay close to the edge of the **Coire Faoin**, while enjoying a new perspective on The Sanctuary. It is a pleasant stroll down across turf cropped short by nature's very own lawnmower, the rabbit!

Before too long, you will reach the burn descending the **Bealach Beag** (**2h35min**). Here, bear left and descend the first few steep metres of the escarpment rocks, taking great care as you do so. Follow the course of the burn to a point lower down, where it turns to flow south. At this point, strike off eastwards across the moor while aiming for the road at the bottom corner of the plantation. Once there, go over a STILE and turn left. It is now just a short walk back along the road to the CAR PARK (**3h15min**).

24 THE QUIRAING

Distance: 6.4km/4mi; 2h35min (not including scrambles up to and over the main rock features)

Grade: a moderately easy short walk with little ascent and following clearly defined, if rough, paths. Things become significantly tougher if you decide to scramble over some of the rock formations, or explore others at close range.

Equipment: 3- or 4-season walking boots or stout shoes. No other special equipment necessary. OS Landranger sheet 23

How to get there and return: 🚗 Park at the higher of the two car parks below the Quiraing (Car tour 8) — or park at the lower one if you fancy more of a climb. 🚌 Local bus from Portree will stop at Brogaig, 3.5km to the east. Nearest accommodation at Staffin, Flodigarry or Uig.

Shorter walk: Walking only as far as the rock formations is an intriguing adventure in itself (1.8km/1.1mi; 1h25min return).

Longer walk: From the 1h20min-point, a barely longer but certainly more strenuous return can be made back over the top of the ridge from Coire Mhic Eachainn, via the summit of Meall na Suiramach above the Quiraing (6.6km/4.1mi; 2h50min).

Because of their proximity to two car parks, and the fact that little effort is involved in reaching them, exploring the fantastic assemblage of pinnacles and pillars at the Quiraing is probably the most popular walk on the Trotternish Peninsula. This Tolkienesque landscape of bracken and detached escarpment rock has been created by the largest ongoing land slippage in Britain. To add to the many virtues of this walk, it is straightforward enough to venture a little beyond the Quiraing, to take in a seaward view of distant islands.

Begin the walk from the HIGHER CAR PARK: take the path going northeast. There is little gradient to tire you. Following the crumbling line of the escarpment, you will en-

counter a number of landslips, but these present no obstacle. The path undulates gently before rising over loose rubble to a point between The Needle, higher up on the left, and the slipped mass of **The Prison** (**45min**), next to you on the right. Both justify closer inspection for those with time and energy.

Gaining the top of The Prison's highest pinnacle is an extremely exciting distraction, but it is only within the grasp of fearless crag-ferrets. Well-practised scrambling skills and an extremely good head

114

The Quiraing, with The Prison on the right

for heights are essential for this little sortie. One begins the climb on The Prison from a worn path ascending its south wall (allow about an extra 25min up and back down).

The main walk continues from The Prison* by heading north along the path that skirts below further basalt monoliths of the Quiraing. It is a unique landscape, sculptured over millions of years by volcano, glacier and ocean; a process which now continues through the imperceptible movements of land slippage.

On crossing a DRYSTONE WALL (**1h05min**), aim for the pinnacles on the skyline ahead, those rising just northwest of **Leac nan Fionn**. An easy path continues north to bring you close to them. Follow it up onto the rim of the **Coire Mhic Eachainn** (**1h20min**). From here, you have a wonderful view over the north tip of Trotternish, out across the Minch as far as the Outer Hebrides and to where a distant horizon meets the sky.

Retrace your footsteps back through the Quiraing to return to the CAR PARK (**2h35min**). From The Prison, you can vary your return slightly by walking down to the lower car park, then following the road back up.

*Before continuing, you might like to take another adventurous detour. From The Prison a very steep slope leads up to **The Needle**. Pass to the left of it and from here go through a breach in the wall of the Quiraing, eventually finding a way up onto a flat grassy area known as **The Table**. Here, cattle were once hidden from pillaging Norsemen, while in more peaceful times, it has been used as a shinty pitch! Return to the path the same way, allowing up to an extra hour for this foray.

25 LOCH CORUISK AND GLEN SLIGACHAN

Distance: 21.8km/13.5mi; 7h05min (allow *at least* 8 hours including inevitable stops)

Grade: a long, very strenuous walk involving a total ascent of 550m/1804ft. Possibly the most arduous walk in the book by virtue of the rough terrain and distance covered. One famously-scary manoeuvre requires some nerve. Many easier walks are possible (see below).

Equipment: 3- or 4-season walking boots and wind/waterproofs. Pack adequate food and water supplies. No other special equipment necessary. OS Landranger sheet 32

How to get there and return: This is a one-way walk. Therefore, ⛟ park at Sligachan (Car tour 8) in the early morning, to catch the Skyeways 🚌 bus to Broadford, then the Postbus to Elgol, walking back to Sligachan. Alternatively, begin from either end of the walk and spend the night at Sligachan Hotel or at a B&B in Elgol, walking back the next day.

Shorter walks: Smaller sections of the main walk can be included in a variety of possible shorter walks:

1 Bypass The Bad Step and Loch Coruisk by continuing north from Camasunary through Strath na Crèitheach (18.2km/11.3mi; 6h).
2 Walk to Loch Coruisk from Kilmarie via the track over Am Màm pass (16.6km/10.3mi; 5h30min return).
3 From Sligachan venture into Glen Sligachan as far as you like before returning.

It would be easy to devise your own short walk using the low-level paths and tracks marked on OS maps.

The Cuillin of Skye is, by common consent, the grandest mountain range in the British Isles. Attaining any one of its jagged peaks involves tough challenges which, together with navigational problems and unreliable compass readings (due to iron in the rock), places just about all routes on them beyond the parameters of this book.

Arduous scrambling and climbing over hard, bare rock is the order of the day on the Black Cuillin — so called because of the black gabbro from which this range is formed.

Mountain summits aside, our route includes probably the finest coastal walk in Britain, visits a remote loch in the most spectacular setting imaginable and provides an ever-changing perspective on the awe-inspiring Cuillin.

Start the walk at **Elgol** where, from the jetty in summer, boat trips across Loch Scavaig provide the opportunity for non-walkers to appreciate the true grandeur of the

The Cuillin of Skye, from Sligachan

mountains close up. From the CUILLIN VIEW TEA ROOM, above the primary school, walk up the B8083 and then turn left along a driveway signposted 'PUBLIC FOOTPATH TO CAMASUNARY AND SLIGACHAN'. Between the LAST TWO HOUSES (**10min**), the undulating footpath continues north above the sea at **Loch Scavaig**, with an outstanding backdrop of mountain scenery. Be especially careful when walking below the cliffs of **Càrn Mór** (**35min**), where the ground drops away sharply to the sea on your left.

Having descended to the beach at the bottom of **Glen Scaladal** (**50min**), pick up the coast path which rises on the far side. Once again, you will need to pay more attention to where you are placing your feet than to the view! Keep a look-out above the hazel and birch scrub for hen harriers, a bird of prey fascinating to watch and frequently observed on Skye.

At **Camasunary Bay**, join a track descending the pass of **Am Màm** on your right, and cross the bridge over the **Abhainn nan Leac** (**1h45min**). Follow the track between the buildings and continue west from where the direct path to Sligachan goes north. Beyond the BOTHY, cross the **Abhainn Camas Fhionnairigh** (**2h**) at stepping stones located about 250m upstream from the beach. If the water is running high, you might just have to wade in up to your knees (or consider the 'Shorter walks').

From the opposite bank, turn south and follow a rugged and often wet, but clearly-defined path around the

headland at **Rubha Bàn (2h 25min)**.

The coastal path continues northwest. The islands of Rum and Soay can be seen across the sea, but it is the close proximity of the imposing mountains that is more likely to bring about a sense of excitement. The adrenaline begins to surge on confronting **The Bad Step (3h10min)**! This manoeuvre in fact involves no more than an easy scramble, first along a level rock ledge, followed by the ascent of a narrow cleft running diagonally for a few metres across a wall of rock. The Bad Step's notoriety can probably be attributed to an almost vertical drop (about 20m/60ft) to the sea, and so the obstacle is more a psychological one. But the rewards so far have been such that, even if forced to retreat from The Bad Step, you will have enjoyed a truly memorable coastal walk amidst scenery not unlike that of a Norwegian fjord. For those of you who successfully negotiated The Bad Step, the best is yet to come.

Walk down across boulders and then around the back of a small beach at the head of **Loch nan Leachd**. Bear right through a CAIRN-MARKED GAP between outcrops of rock to reach the shore of wild **Loch Coruisk (3h25min)**. The experience of being almost completely encircled by the sensational skyline of the Cuillin in this, the remotest of settings, is breathtaking. The artists
118

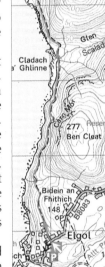

among you will appreciate why the painter Turner was so inspired here, lured not only by the unique drama of the place, but no doubt also by the shifting quality of the light.

Leave Loch Coruisk by continuing at first on the path along its east shore but, within a few minutes, bear northeast up a path beside the stream, to reach its source at **Loch a' Choire Riabhaich (4h10min)**. From here, continue your ascent more steeply, until you emerge on the ridge at the top of the path. This superb vantage point, just below **Sgurr Hain (4h35min)**, offers yet another fine perspective on the Cuillin. The wonderful sight of Bla Bheinn, as well as the 'Red Cuillin', are also the just rewards for your efforts.

A good path allows you to descend easily on the north side. At the bottom join the main path through **Glen Sligachan (5h 25min)**. Ahead of you is a long but straight-forward hike through the glen. A gentle descent on the well-used path, in good condition for most of the way, follows the river between the sharp peaks of Sgurr nan Gillean and the Black Cuillin on one side, and Marsco and the smoothly-rounded Red Cuillin on the other — so called because of the pink granite from which this less-imposing range is formed.

At the bottom of the glen, the path ends at the old BRIDGE (**7h05min**) by the parking area. The SLIGACHAN HOTEL beckons with the promise of a hearty meal and a wee dram or two; no better motivation for tired legs.

26 COIRE MHIC FHEARCHAIR (BEINN EIGHE)

Distance: 13km/8mi; 4h15min

Grade: a moderate-strenuous walk involving an ascent of 525m/1722ft. Nowhere is the climb too steep, although the path in its upper reaches traverses difficult terrain.

Equipment: 3- or 4-season walking boots, wind/waterproofs and some food. No other special equipment necessary. OS Landranger sheets 19 and 25

How to get there and return: 🚗 Park in the main Glen Torridon car park, between Beinn Eighe and Liathach (Car tour 9). 🚌 Served by Achnasheen to Diabaig Postbus. Nearest accommodation: YH in Torridon, the Torridon Hotel and at Kinlochewe.

Shorter walks: Park in the small parking bay 2km east of the main Glen Torridon car park and ascend the good stalkers' path beside the burn draining Coire an Laoigh. Walk up to the lip of this corrie (370m/1214ft; 1h30min up and back down). Stronger climbers can continue to the summit of Spidean Coire nan Clach (867m/2844ft; 4h up and down), the most easily-accessible peak on Beinn Eighe.

Longer walk: Having returned to the junction of paths on the way down from Loch Coire Mhic Fhearchair, turn right and follow the path around the north side of Liathach to its terminus at the Coire Mhic Nòbuil (535m/1755ft; 5h15min). You will need to organise transport back to your car.

Beinn Eighe is the easternmost mountain of the wonderful Torridonian triptych, distinguished by its liberal covering of quartzite scree which gives the effect of it being permanently snow-capped. Together with Liathach and Beinn Alligin, Beinn Eighe proves an irresistible magnet for hillwalkers and Munro-baggers. To reach any of the peaks of these challenging mountains, however, involves a considerable challenge. The toughest test of all is mighty Liathach, out of bounds to all but the most daring and competent.

Fortunately, the best feature of Beinn Eighe, the fabulous Coire Mhic Fhearchair, is well within the capabilities of all reasonably-fit walkers. And that is the goal of this walk — one of the finest corries in the Scottish Highlands, revealing a truly awesome display of mountain architecture.

Start the walk at the MAIN CAR PARK in **Glen Torridon**, by the bridge. Walk up the well-trodden but well-preserved, gradually rising path which keeps to the left side of the **Allt Coire an Anmoich**. The view ahead of you is dominated by an extensive scree-smothered wall, soaring skyward at Beinn Eighe's western extremity. As you gain more height, the overwhelming sandstone cliffs and terraces of Liathach, which loom above you on your left, are no less intimidating — inviting none but the bravest to attempt an ascent. Step easily over an intervening BURN (**30min**), where it is worth just pausing for a while, to take it all, here in eagle country and among some of the oldest mountains on earth.

Where the gap between Liathach and Beinn Eighe approaches its narrowest, up in the **Coir Dubh Mor**, cross the river on STEPPING STONES (**50min**). On your left is a large boulder split by the forces of nature but giving the impression of having been sliced with a giant knife, so conspicuously precise is the divide. Few other distinctive

The Triple Buttress, seen from across Loch Coire Mhic Fhearchair

features of reference exist in this primeval landscape. However, the path remains clearly evident and the gradient eases.

Near **Lochan a' Choire Dhuibh**, a CAIRN (**1h15min**) marks the point where the path divides. You now have a fantastic perspective on Liathach's dramatic north side, as well as to the previously-hidden mountains, Beinn Alligin and Beinn Dearg. From here, take the fork to the right, skirting below Sàil Mhor. Ascending this wetter, irregular and in places bouldery terrain, your pace is inevitably slowed. From a CAIRN (**1h25min**) located on rock slabs, you have a fine view down over Loch nan Caber. Soon the vastness of this primeval landscape is seen to best effect, as you look across the *lochan*-pitted Flowerdale Forest (a forest of neither flowers nor trees!), towards Beinn an Eòin (**1h35min**).

Having progressed further, be sure to take special care when stepping across a succession of large boulders, if twisting your ankle is to be avoided! Continuing along the path, you are soon making your way steeply up between outcrops which, in themselves, are worthy of closer inspection. On some of the quartzite can be found numerous fossilised worm burrows, among the earliest traces of life known in Scotland.

Stay to the right of the river where you pass a prominent WATERFALL (**2h10min**). Looming above you now, on your right, are the two huge cathedral-like sandstone domes of **Sàil Mhór**. A short stroll above the waterfall will find you at the shore of **Loch Coire Mhic Fhearchair** (**2h15min**), its waters cradled, but not lovingly so, by a surround of imposing buttresses of rock and elevated ridges.

The most distinctive feature of the Coire Mhic Fhearchair is, undoubtedly, the awe-inspiring **Triple Buttress**. To best appreciate these three magnificent castellated towers of rock, venture a little further east along the north shore of the loch. You may then view them directly across the water, a memorable site in an exceptional corner of wilderness! The feeling of remoteness, a world away from the cares of civilisation, could not be more profound.

From the Coire Mhic Fhearchair, it is feasible for strong, capable and properly-prepared hillwalkers to climb Ruadh-Stac Mór, the highest of Beinn Eighe's summits and the peak rising immediately to your left. From there, the view extends far beyond Loch Maree, to the remotest mountains of Scotland, to the Great Wilderness of Letterewe. However, those of you pursuing a more modest endeavour can return in the certain knowledge that you have not missed out in any way. Retrace your footsteps back to the CAR PARK in the glen (**4h15min**).

27 BEINN ALLIGIN

Distance: 6km/3.7mi; 3h50min

Grade: a strenuous and steep ascent of 882m/2893ft, traversing tough terrain, but with no technical difficulty and not too long. Competence with a compass is advisable (see notes on 'Walking').

Equipment: 3- or 4-season walking boots and wind/waterproofs; waterproof gaiters would come in handy. OS Landranger sheet 24

How to get there and return: 🚇 Park in the car park on west side of the bridge over the Abhainn Coire Mhic Nòbuil, below Beinn Alligin (Car tour 9). 🚌 Served by Achnasheen to Diabaig Postbus. Nearest accommodation as for Walk 26, page 120.

Shorter walks: From the car park indicated above, head west along the minor road for 500m, then take the path off to the left, to the shore of the loch. Visit lovely Torridon Kirk and continue west along the shore of Upper Loch Torridon, as far as Alligin Shuas, returning by the quiet little road below Beinn Alligin (9km/5.6mi; 2h30min). Alternatively, wander up the good path on right bank of Abhainn Coire Mhic Nòbuil as far as you like.

Longer walks: Competent walkers who enjoy light scrambling can continue to Beinn Alligin's Munro summit, Sgurr Mhór, before returning (9km/5.6mi; 6h). Very capable scramblers might continue still further, on an entertaining traverse of Na Rathanan, the three castellated pinnacles known as the Horns of Alligin. Descend southeast from the last of them, completing a strenuous circuit (10km/6.2mi; 6h30min). One further possibility is as for 'Longer walk' on page 120, but in reverse.

If you are new to the Torridon mountains and feel compelled to climb a high mountain, then try Beinn Alligin first. Of the Torridonian triptych, it is the least complex mountain and the easiest to climb. Although more forgiving than either Beinn Eighe or Liathach, it shares many of the same features which characterise these giants.

Beinn Alligin has long narrow ridges which connect its various summits, interspersed with formidable castellated tiers of red Torridonian sandstone and patches of quartzite scree. But there is perhaps just one summit among them, Tom na Gruagaich, which avoids altogether the difficulties that are typical of Torridon's arduous high-level ridges. By my reckoning, it also happens to be one of the finest viewpoints in the Scottish Highlands.

Before setting off, first take a little time to view the scene upstream from the bridge, enjoying the pine-fringed cascades of

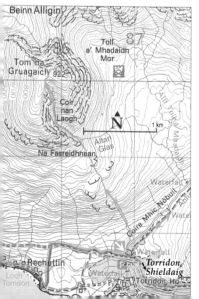

Sgurr Mhór (the main summit of Beinn Alligin), from the approach to Tom na Gruagaich. Na Rathanan (The Horns) can be seen in the distance.

the **Abhainn Coire Mhic Nòbuil**, a green and tranquil oasis in an otherwise rather bleak surround of austere mountain slopes. Then **begin the walk** on the wet path on the west side of the BRIDGE, soon leaving the river behind while heading north across the steeply-rising moor. The going is not easy, in many places bouldery and feature-less, but navigation should not be a problem.

Make your way towards the gap between the outcrops that are directly below the rounded summit ahead. Here, at the foot of the **Coir' nan Laogh**, a path ascends the left side of a burn, the **Altan Glas (1h)**. Bear left and follow the path, climbing steeply up into the corrie which becomes increasingly confined the higher you go. Stay on the left side of the burn, all the way up to its source, paying particular attention on loose and slippery rocks. I have seen ptarmigan up here on more than one occasion, and should you happen to come upon one too, then you are probably at least 700m above sea level.

Just as the steep climb out of the corrie is beginning to feel like a relentless slog, you gain the flat TOP (**1h50min**) of a broad ridge. Bear right and walk northeast across this much easier, moss-covered high ground to reach the TRIG PILLAR ON **Tom na Gruagaich (2h)**. The views, far-reaching in all directions, are quite simply breathtaking. On the seaward horizon is the Isle of Skye, while Liathach, Beinn Eighe and a closer neighbour, Beinn Dearg, can be seen to the east, with the isolated mountain of Baosbhein dominating Shieldaig Forest to the north. Looking across to Sgurr Mhòr, the highest of Beinn Alligin's summits, you can observe the tremendous gash known as Eag Dhubh (the black cleft). Scotland's last wolf is said to have in-habited the corrie below it. The display is unforgettable — a profoundly beautiful wilderness, but a landscape where perhaps human beings have no place for too long.

You should return from Tom na Gruagaich by your ascent route (**3h50min**) unless the lure of the Munro sum-mit, The Horns, and a sporting ridge walk and scramble, proves too irresistible (see 'Longer Walks').

125

28 THE MAINNRICHEAN BUTTRESS OF FUAR THOLL

Distance: 11km/6.8mi; 4h15min

Grade: A moderate and straightforward walk following good paths on an ascent of 650m/2132ft.

Equipment: 3- or 4-season walking boots and wind/waterproofs, but no other special equipment necessary. OS Landranger sheet 25

How to get there and return: 🚗 Park at the parking bay opposite the private road leading up to Achnashellach Station (Car tour 9). 🚃 Trains operating between Inverness and Kyle of Lochalsh stop here. Nearest accommodation: Strathcarron and Lochcarron.

Shorter walks: Simply return at any point once you have walked far enough into the Coire Làir.

Longer walks: Continuing to the summit of Fuar Tholl is an option only for those who have come properly prepared (see notes on 'Walking'). Climb up steeply southeast from the top of the pass at the 2h15min-point to reach the trig pillar. Return the same way (14km/8.7mi; 5h45min). A more direct, but very steep and pathless descent is possible via the southeast slopes (10km/6.2mi; 4h30min). There are also two options for through walks, heading north to Glen Torridon from Achnashellach, for those not needing to return to a car. Glen Torridon is served by Achnasheen to Diabaig Postbus.

1   Continue north, to climb the uppermost reaches of Coire Làir, going over the Bealach Bàn, followed by the Bealach na Lice, finally descending to Annat (17.7km/11mi; 7h).

2   A shorter and easier option than (1) above involves less ascent and uses a good track through the Coulin Pass, descending to Loch Coulin and Loch Clair (12.9km/8mi; 4h30min).

Thanks to a network of good deer-stalkers' paths which penetrate the Coulin Forest, those of you feeling especially fit and energetic can complete a traverse of the mountainous country between Glen Torridon and Glen Carron by tackling one of the 'Longer Walks' above. However, a shorter and more straightforward excursion utilises two good paths ascending Coire Làir, bringing the unique and awesome tower of Torridonian sandstone known as the Mainnrichean Buttress of Fuar Tholl to within range of everyone with enough energy.

Fuar Tholl is an impressive mountain and probably the one most worth visiting in the Coulin Forest. It looms high and with threatening menace above the road in Glen Carron, but do not let that put you off. There is nothing to cause you concern if you are only visiting the buttress.

Start the walk from the PARKING BAY opposite the private road to Achnashellach Station. Walk up to the STATION (**5min**), go across the railway, and follow a track uphill for a further 100 metres. Then turn left on another forestry track and continue along it until an ARROW points down to a KISSING GATE by the bank of the **River Lair** (**20min**).

From here, walk upstream along the river, towards the imposing rocky heights of Fuar Tholl.

On reaching an Achnashellach Estate SIGN (**30min**) warning of deer stalking activities between '15th September and 20th October', you are now on the open moor above the forestry trees. Here, native pines cling to the side of a lovely GORGE on your left (**35min**). Higher up, the quality of the path deteriorates somewhat, but it remains clearly defined. You cannot get lost here.

The Mainnrichean Buttress of Fuar Tholl

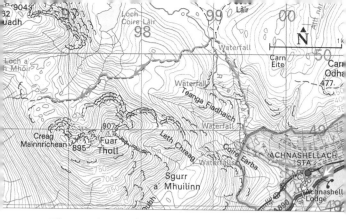

The gradient relents on arriving at the wide basin of
Coire Làir (**55min**), having now climbed well above Glen
Carron. A CAIRN (**1h05min**) marks the junction of paths in
this corrie, a lonely place surrounded by the very highest
mountains of the Coulin Forest. The mountaineers among
you might well be tempted by the challenge of the long
ridge traverse all the way around the corrie skyline.

Turn left and walk down to ford the RIVER (**1h10min**),
normally an insignificant obstacle. From the opposite
bank, you can sustain a fair walking pace on an undulating path which crosses an intriguing landscape, the
ground here littered with boulders and pitted with tiny
pools and *lochans*. All intervening burns are easily
crossed, and the climb is a gentle one, with the uplifting
view ahead of Fuar Tholl's east-facing cliffs.

When you come below the NORTH-FACING CLIFFS (**1h
35min**), the gradient steepens appreciably. Below you,
on your right, is **Loch Coire Làir**, but it is the presence of
the Mainnrichean Buttress that commends your attention
from here on. When seen from below, the scree slopes
on either side of this tremendous upthrust of Torridonian
sandstone make it seem isolated from the main bulk of
the mountain. The buttress is best appreciated from the
tiny burn draining the '**Cold Hollow**' (**2h**), but it is also
reflected well in the waters of a tiny *lochan* a little further
up (**2h05min**). From here, it is obvious why the **Mainnrichean Buttress** is very much a rock climbers' peak.

It is worth the little extra effort to walk on up to the TOP
OF THE PASS (**2h15min**), to look down on the valley below
and for a better view of the mountains of Ben-Damph
Forest. From here retrace your outgoing route back to the
PARKING BAY (**4h15min**).

29 SUILVEN

See also photograph page 133   **Distance:** 18km/11.2mi; 7h

Grade: a very strenuous route involving a long walk followed by a steep ascent. Total height gain is 755m/2476ft, not including any optional scrambling on the ridge. Competence with a compass is advisable (see notes on 'Walking').

Equipment: 3- or 4-season walking boots and wind/waterproofs; take plenty of food. OS Landranger sheet 15

How to get there and return: 🚗 Park at end of the minor road, near Glencanisp Lodge, 1.7km/1mi east of the A837 at Lochinver (Car tour 10). 🚌 Lochinver has a weekly bus connection with Inverness; also served by the Lochinver/Drumbeg Postbus. Plenty of accommodation in Lochinver.

Shorter walks: The approach to Suilven from Glencanisp is a very fine walk in itself. Turn back at any point along the stalkers' path, before the ascent of Suilven begins. A lovely circular walk from Lochinver follows the path going upstream along the River Inver, before striking south across the wild moor to Glencanisp Lodge and then west by the minor road back to the village (8.3km/5.2mi; 2h45min).

Longer walks: Capable scramblers should find continuing over the pinnacles of Suilven's ridge, going eastwards to the summit of Meall Meadonach from the Bealach Mór, a very enjoyable extension to the main route (20km/12.4mi; 7h50min). Another alternative would be a return to Lochinver via the River Inver (the reverse of the suggestion for 'Shorter walks'), especially suitable for those who begin the main walk from the village (23km/14.3mi; 8h20min).

Perforated by numerous lochs and *lochans,* the Assynt landscape is one almost as much of water as it is of land. However, it is the mountains which make this part of the Northwest Highlands so distinctive and, of all the weird and wonderful isolated shapes which rise above the Sutherland moors, Suilven is the grandest. The usual approach for walkers attempting the challenge of Suilven is from Lochinver, but you must be prepared for a long walk across untamed country before the ascent begins.

Walkers on the ridge path of Suilven, near the summit

Start the walk from the END OF THE MINOR ROAD, 1km west of Glencanisp Lodge. From here, you will see just why Suilven was known to the Vikings as 'Pillar Mountain' and why today many refer to it as the 'Sugar Loaf'. Walk east past GLENCANISP LODGE (**15min**), and go through a green iron gate, to gain an unmetalled track leading to the far east end of **Loch Druim Suardalain (20min)**. The track narrows to a footpath between dense thickets of gorse and, in spring, a carpet of bluebells.

The pretty flowers soon give way to open moorland, a terrain characterised by rugged gneiss outcrops, peaty quagmires and innumerable dark pools of water. Fortunately, an excellent stalkers' path avoids you having to endure what would otherwise be an arduous trek over ground ridden with obstacles.

Like Suilven, Canisp is a detached mountain and is soon seen directly ahead of you. As you progress, more of Suilven's craggy ridge is revealed, and the new profile, resembling the shape of a beached galleon, defies early impressions of the mountain.

Undulating between outcrops, the path divides at **Suileag (1h30min)**. Take the right-hand fork and continue towards Canisp, passing beside a DRYSTONE WALL and then coming alongside the **Abhainn na Clach Airigh**. For those of you who enjoy isolation, the rewards of this wilderness will already be keenly felt. Suilven is one of the more popular hillwalks in the region, but it is never busy. Here, you can revel in the joy of being alone without, let's hope, getting lost!

Follow the river upstream to **Lochan Buidhe (2h)**, just beyond which the path divides again. Turn right and go over the FOOTBRIDGE (**2h05min**), to gain the path heading southwards at first. But strike off southwest (**2h15min**) on a rougher path which makes a beeline for Suilven. Steeper and harder walking is involved where you cross the slushy peat that leads up to level ground at **Loch a' Choire Dhuibh (2h55min)**, immediately below Suilven. Whilst from here the mountain would appear to be an unbreachable fortress, CAIRNS from the west side of the loch guide you to the bottom of a very steep stony gully. Climb this directly, all the way to the TOP OF THE **Bealach Mór (3h40min)**.

On arriving at the ridge, you realise that your persistence has all been worthwhile: the views across Inverpolly Nature Reserve are exceptional. For a more extensive panorama, turn right and walk along the ridge path towards the main summit. This involves only easy scrambling, but you will find yourself in one or two exposed situations, before emerging on the grassy table-top plateau of **Caisteal Liath**, **Suilven's** HIGHEST SUMMIT (731m/2398ft; **4h**). Having climbed up from the *bealach,* you will have passed through a gap in a drystone wall. This wall (photograph page 129) straddles the ridge like a saddle over a horse's back, and its purpose completely defies explanation!

The view from Suilven is across a remarkable wilderness. It is almost like another planet, watery but very beautiful and, if you listen carefully, you might just hear a red-throated diver, its eerie call emanating from any one of a number of tiny *lochans.* Among the many distinctive mountains to be seen is Stac Pollaidh (Walk 30; see photograph page 133), while looking seaward beyond an indented coastline, lie The Minch and the Atlantic.

Scramblers might well wish to venture to Suilven's eastern summit, Meall Meadhonach, before heading back down. Those who have enjoyed quite enough excitement for one day should return to the Bealach Mór and retrace their steps back to Glencanisp Lodge (**7h**).

30 STAC POLLAIDH (STACK POLLY)

See STOP PRESS on page 136

Distance: 3km/1.9mi; 2h

Grade: a very short but moderate-strenuous walk involving an extremely sharp ascent of 533m/1748ft, with optional scrambling along the summit ridge.

Equipment: 3- or 4-season walking boots and wind/waterproofs. No navigational problems are likely (but see notes on 'Walking'). OS Landranger sheet 15

How to get there and return: 🚗 Park in the car park above Loch Lurgainn, at the southern edge of Inverpolly Forest (Car tour 10). 🚌 The nearest bus drop-off point is at Drumrunie (8km/5mi to the southeast), but more frequent Postbuses serve Elphin (16km/10mi to the east) and Lochinver. Nearest accommodation at Elphin and Lochinver.

Longer walks: Although it is difficult to find, a steep path descends from the low point of the summit ridge on the northeast side of the mountain, before turning back south, allowing variation and a slightly longer return. A further alternative is a substantially longer but straightforward mountain walk in the Inverpolly NNR: climb Cul Mor from the Knockan Visitor Centre (9.5km/5.9mi; 4h30min). Another option is the traverse of Stack Polly's porcupine ridge; this involves some difficult but exciting scrambling over a succession of exposed sandstone pinnacles, to reach both the west and east summits (4km/2.4mi; 3h).

Stac Pollaidh (usually anglicised to Stack Polly) is Scotland's 'porcupine' mountain, a monolith raising its sandstone hackles above the wilds of Assynt. It is something of a dwarf compared to its neighbours, but so striking is its appearance, that it assumes a presence which far exceeds its stature. The route to the low point on the summit ridge is the shortest and most straightforward walk in this book, but the climb is extremely sharp. The optional scrambling thereafter involves tricky manoeuvres which, in places, comes close to rock climbing, should you wish to take it on!

Stack Polly is a popular hill walk, and a car park has been built off the minor road lying directly south of the mountain, just above the shore of Loch Lurgainn. **Start out** at this CAR PARK: cross the road and take the clear, well-maintained footpath which leads up to a flatter, muddier area. Take the LEFT FORK (**15min**) where the path divides, continuing ever more steeply up the grassy hillside that has become eroded by a succession of hillwalkers. A series of deep muddy trenches have been eroded along this route that makes no compromise towards a less direct way to the top. Navigation along this clearly-defined path

Looking across Inverpolly from Suilven, to Stac Pollaidh in the centre distance

is easy, but it will leave you breathless. Your ordeal is quite brief, and a final clamber below towering pinnacles leads up to the narrow, shattered SUMMIT RIDGE ON **Stack Polly** (**1h10min**).

This low point in the summit ridge offers truly stunning views to the east, to the other outlying atolls of the Inverpolly NNR, Cul Mor and Cul Beag, as well as to Suilven (Walk 29) and north Assynt. The extensive sheet of water and birch-clad islands of Loch Sionascaig, the mountains nearby, the fragmented woodlands and vast spread of undulating moorland extending to the sea, together make up what is Britain's second largest NNR. The flora and fauna of the reserve are outstanding because of the wide range of habitats that are present, from marine islands to barren mountaintops, where seabirds, otters, ptarmigan and rare mountain plants can be seen.

Stack Polly is a scramblers' paradise and venturing along the summit ridge is not for the faint-hearted. There also exists a maze of easier paths below the rock serrations which line the crest of the ridge heading over to the west summit. However, whichever route you take will bring you to exposed but sensational situations amid spectacular pinnacles and towers of rock. You will find that gaining the east summit is a marginally easier ordeal, but many of you will have found quite enough fulfilment on simply arriving at the ridge.

A knee-jarring descent is unavoidable. Return the same way to the CAR PARK (**2h**) and be sure to glance back over your shoulder to what you are leaving behind. There is nothing like it in all of Britain.

Index

Geographical names comprise the only entries in this Index. For other entries, see Contents, page 3. **Bold type** indicates a photograph; *italic* type a map.

USEFUL ADDRESSES

Tourist boards

Argyll, the Isles, Loch Lomond, Stirling & Trossachs Tourist Board
Old Town Jail, St John Street
Stirling FK8 1EA
Tel: 01786 470945

Fort William and Lochaber Tourist Board
Cameron Square
Fort William PH33 6AJ
Tel: 01379 703781

Highlands of Scotland Tourist Board
Peffery House
Strathpeffer IV14 9HA
Tel: 01997 421160

Scottish Tourist Board
23 Ravelston Terrace
Edinburgh EH4 3EU
Tel: 0131 332 2433

Bus and rail services

Midland Bluebird
(for bus service to Crianlarich)
Stirling
Tel: 01324 623901

National Coach Services
(National Express enquiry line)
Tel: 0990 808080

Postbus
(contact number for timetables)
Royal Mail Public Relations Office
Edinburgh
Tel: 0131 228 7407

ScotRail Customer Services
(for Edinburgh, Glasgow, West Highland line services)
Tel: 0141 3354612
(train information)
Tel: 0345 484950

Miscellaneous

Forestry Commission
231 Corstorphine Road
Edinburgh EH12 7AT
Tel: 0131 334 0303

The Mountaineering Council of Scotland
4a St Catherine's Road
Perth PH1 5SE
Tel: 01738 638227

National Trust for Scotland
5 Charlotte Square
Edinburgh EH2 4DU
Tel: 0131 226 5922

Royal Society for the Protection of Birds (RSPB)
Scottish Headquarters
17 Regent Street
Edinburgh EH7 5BN
Tel: 0131 557 3136

Scottish Avalance Information Service (SAIS)
Police/SAIS Avalanche
Information Line
Tel: 01479 861264

Scottish Natural Heritage (SNH)
12 Hope Terrace
Edinburgh EH9 2AS
Tel: 0131 447 4784

Scottish Wildlife Trust (SWT)
Cramond House
Cramond Glebe Road
Edinburgh EH4 6NS
Tel: 0131 312 7765

Scottish Youth Hostels Association (SYHA)
7 Glebe Crescent
Stirling FK8 2JA
Tel: 01786 451181

STOP PRESS

Walk 30: At press date Scottish Natural Heritage have just begun urging walkers to avoid the well-worn path up the south side of Stac Pollaidh (the route described in the book), claiming that excessive erosion has rendered the path dangerous. The route marked to the east and north of the summit (shown in dashed lines on the map) is currently being upgraded. Longer-term plans are to create a circular path round the mountain.